Developing Numeracy

CALCULATIONS

ACTIVITIES FOR THE DAILY MATHS LESSON

year 5

Dave Kirkby

A & C BLACK

Contents

Rapid recall of multiplication and division facts

Mental calculation strategies (x and ÷)

Pencil and paper procedures (x, ÷, + and –)

Resources

Answers

Reprinted 2002

Published 2002 by A & C Black Publishers Limited

37 Soho Square, London W1D 3QZ

www.acblack.com

ISBN 0-7136-6056-2

Editors: Lynne Williamson and Marie Lister

The author and publishers would like to thank Madeleine Madden and Corinne McCrum for their advice in producing this series of books.

A CIP catalogue record for this book is available from the British Library.

A & C Black uses paper produced with elemental chlorine-free pulp, harvested from managed sustainable forests.

Printed in Great Britain by Caligraving Ltd, Thetford, Norfolk.

Introduction

Developing Numeracy: Calculations is a series of seven photocopiable activity books designed to be used during the daily maths lesson. They focus on the second strand of the National Numeracy Strategy *Framework for teaching mathematics*. The activities are intended to be used in the time allocated to pupil activities; they aim to reinforce the knowledge, understanding and skills taught during the main part of the lesson and to provide practice and consolidation of the objectives contained in the framework document.

Year 5 supports the teaching of mathematics by providing a series of activities which develop important calculation skills. On the whole the activities are designed for children to work on independently, although this is not always possible and occasionally some children may need support.

Year 5 encourages children to:

- derive addition pairs to 100, and pairs of multiples of 50 to 1000, and pairs of one-place decimals to 1 and 10;
- calculate mentally differences by counting up through the next multiple of 10, 100 or 1000;
- add several single-digit numbers, and multiples of 10, using different strategies;
- use known number facts and place value to add or subtract mentally, including any pair of three-digit multiples of 10;
- use informal written methods for HTU +/− HTU, ThHTU +/− HTU;
- use standard written methods for HTU + HTU, ThHTU + HTU, addition of more than two such numbers, and addition of decimal numbers (both with one or both with two decimal places);
- use standard written methods for HTU − HTU, and subtraction of decimal numbers (both with one or both with two decimal places);
- know by heart all multiplication facts up to 10 x 10;
- derive division facts from multiplication facts;
- begin to express a quotient as a fraction or as a decimal when dividing a whole number by 2, 4, 5 or 10;
- derive doubles of whole numbers to 100, multiples of 10 to 1000, multiples of 100 to 10 000; and all corresponding halves;
- use standard written methods for short multiplication of HTU x U or U.t x U;
- use standard written methods for long multiplication of TU x TU;
- use standard written methods for short division of HTU ÷ U (with whole number remainder).

Extension

Many of the activity sheets end with a challenge (**Now try this!**) which reinforces and extends the children's learning, and provides the teacher with the opportunity for assessment. On occasion it may be necessary to read the instructions with the children before they begin the activity. For some of the challenges the children will need to record their answers on a separate piece of paper.

Organisation

Very little equipment is needed, but it will be useful to have available: coloured pencils, counters, scissors, calculators and dice. Children may need number lines, 1–100 number squares and multiplication squares. These can be used to model mental calculations, but encourage the children to calculate without using them wherever possible.

Other useful counting equipment includes interlocking cubes, coins, base ten material, place-value boards, and number cards (which are provided on page 61). Ideally a variety of different types of apparatus should be used to help children understand concepts and develop mathematical language.

The activities in this book will naturally bring in elements of counting and problem solving. Children need to be confident and efficient in counting to be able to develop their calculation skills effectively. They will need regular counting practice to consolidate and develop the skills outlined in the Numbers and the Number System strand of the Strategy for Year 5 (see **Developing Numeracy: Numbers and the Number System Year 5**).

To help teachers select appropriate learning experiences for the children, the activities are grouped into sections within this book. However, the activities are not expected to be used in that order; the sheets are intended to support, rather than direct, the teacher's planning. Some activities are deliberately more challenging than others, to allow for the widely varying ability in most classrooms. Many activities can be made easier or more challenging by masking and substituting some of the numbers. You may wish to re-use some pages by copying them onto card and laminating them, or by enlarging them onto A3 paper.

Teachers' notes

Brief notes are provided at the foot of each page giving ideas and suggestions for maximising the effectiveness of the activity sheets. These can be masked before copying.

Notes on calculation methods

Multiplication

Common practice is to describe the x sign as 'lots of' (which younger children find easier to understand), rather than the more precise 'multiplied by'. This 'lots of' approach has the effect of reversing the repeated addition: for example, 3 multiplied by 4 (3 + 3 + 3 + 3) becomes 3 lots of 4 (4 + 4 + 4). What is critical in the teaching of multiplication is the fact that the order of multiplication does not matter, i.e. 3 x 4 = 4 x 3. If this is done it matters less which method is taught.

A school needs to decide whether to initially teach multiplication using 'lots of' to describe the x sign or the slightly more mathematical 'multiplied by'. Throughout this series, multiplication is treated as 'lots of' for continuity.

Checking results

Calculators are a valuable and essential aid in developing calculation skills and can be used to provide immediate feedback to children as to whether or not a particular calculation is correct.

Children should be encouraged to use other checking procedures besides calculators. Many activities allow for checking by using an inverse operation, for example using division to check a multiplication. This reinforces the links between adding and subtracting, multiplying and dividing, doubling and halving.

Estimation

Encourage the children to acquire the habit of making an estimate before attempting any calculation which cannot be done mentally. This develops rounding skills and gives a sense of the size of the answer. Encourage children always to follow up the calculation by comparing the answer with the estimate.

Recording written calculations

When children attempt written calculations, it is likely that they will be working at different levels. Some may still be using informal methods, whereas others may be ready for more sophisticated methods. It is recommended that the sheets be used flexibly, and adapted to suit the methods appropriate for individual children.

Whole-class warm-up activities

The following activities provide some practical ideas which can be used to introduce the main teaching part of the lesson.

Rapid recall of number facts

Sliding box

Make strips of card, all the same size, each showing a different number fact (for example, make a set showing decimal number pairs that total 10). Make a sliding 'box' by cutting parallel slots in a rectangular piece of card, as shown.

 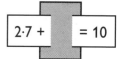

Slide the box to different positions on the strips and ask the children to say the hidden number.

Flash cards

Make sets of cards, each showing a number fact on the front and the answer on the reverse, for example, a set of x8 multiplication facts. The children can use these to practise recalling facts, turning them over to check the answer.

front $\boxed{6 \times 8}$ $\boxed{48}$ reverse

Double-sided practice cards

Make sets of cards to practise doubling and halving skills. For example, for the doubles of the multiples of 10 to 1000, write some of the multiples of 10 in red on one side of the cards, and their corresponding doubles in blue on the other side. Shuffle the cards and arrange them with the red numbers face up to provide a set of random doubling tasks. The children can check the answers by looking at the reverse side. Then place the blue numbers face up to provide halving practice.

Similar sets of cards can be produced for other facts, for example 'multiplying by 8' and 'dividing by 8'.

Multiplication square

A multiplication square can be used to check the first ten multiples of any number. Give the children plenty of practice in reciting the multiples of numbers from 2 to 10. Chant the multiples, both forwards and backwards, first with the multiplication square and then without.

Mental calculation strategies

1 to 100 square

A 1–100 square provides a model for mental addition and subtraction involving two-digit numbers. Moving down a column illustrates adding tens and moving up illustrates subtracting tens. Sliding right illustrates adding ones and sliding left illustrates subtracting ones.

Number lines

Unlabelled 10-point and 100-point number lines are valuable resources for modelling mental addition and subtraction skills. Label the ends of the line with numbers appropriate to the calculation. Addition can be modelled by jumping from left to right along the line (i.e. counting on), and subtraction by jumping from right to left along the line (i.e. counting back). Number lines are also useful for encouraging awareness of the positional sense of numbers, for example one-place decimal numbers 0 to 10.

Snack attack!

- **Write how much change from a £1 coin.**

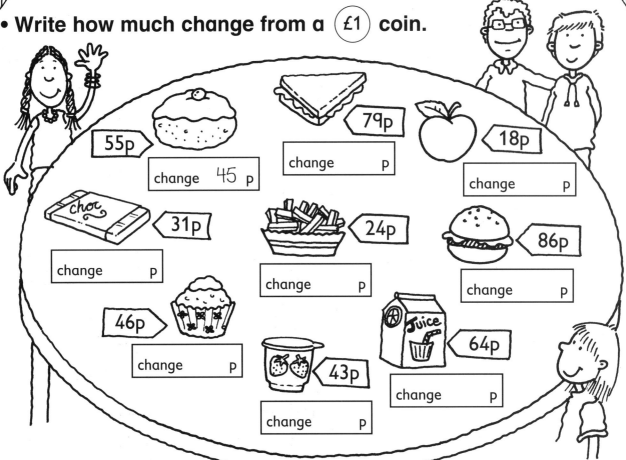

55p

change 45 p

79p

change ___ p

18p

change ___ p

31p

change ___ p

24p

change ___ p

86p

change ___ p

46p

change ___ p

43p

change ___ p

64p

change ___ p

- **The coins show the change from £1. Write how much each item cost.**

Coins used for change	Cost of item	Coins used for change	Cost of item
50p 10p 2p	38p	20p 10p 5p	
50p 5p		20p 10p 10p 1p	
20p 5p 10p 1p		10p 2p 1p	

- **Two numbers total 100. What are the two numbers if:**

the difference between them is 4 _____ _____	one is 28 less than the other _____ _____	one is 16 more than the other _____ _____

Now try this!

Teachers' note The children can model the addition pairs using a 100-point number line, labelled 0 at one end and 100 at the other. Locate a number on the line, for example 37, and read the distance to 100. It can be seen as six tens and three units, i.e. 63. Children commonly make the error of saying that the difference is 73; the use of number lines helps to avoid this.

**Developing Numeracy
Calculations Year 5
© A & C Black**

Thirsty work!

Each child has a drink from a litre carton of juice.

• Write how many millilitres of juice are left.

1 litre is 1000 millilitres.

1. I drank 200 ml
juice
800 ml

2. I drank 700 ml
juice
___ ml

3. I drank 650 ml

juice
___ ml

4. I drank 150 ml

juice
___ ml

5. I drank 850 ml

juice
___ ml

6. I drank 350 ml

juice
___ ml

• These children drink from the same carton. How much is left?

7. I drank 200 ml   I drank 350 ml   ___ ml

8. I drank 150 ml   I drank 650 ml   ___ ml

9. I drank 400 ml   I drank 50 ml   ___ ml

10. I drank $\frac{1}{2}$ l   I drank 150 ml   ___ ml

11. I drank $\frac{1}{4}$ l   I drank 300 ml   ___ ml

12. I drank $\frac{2}{5}$ l   I drank 150 ml   ___ ml

Now try this!

A litre bottle of lemonade has 550 ml left. Jon and Jez drank the same amount each.

• How much did each boy drink? _____ ml

Teachers' note Encourage the children to make the link between pairs of two-digit numbers which total 100, for example 37 and 63, and multiples of 10 which total 1000, such as 370 and 630. As a further extension, the children can set each other more 'Thirsty work' problems. Ensure they have worked out the answers themselves first.

Developing Numeracy Calculations Year 5 © A & C Black

Hole in one game

• Play this game with a partner.

☆ Mix up the counters. Place one on each ball.

☆ Decide who is going to be which colour.

☆ Take turns to remove a counter in your colour. Find the matching 'hole' to make **10**.

☆ If your partner agrees, cover the hole with your counter. If not, put the counter back on the ball.

☆ The winner is the first to cover five holes.

You need
24 counters
(12 in one colour, 12 in another).

Teachers' note Encourage the children to make the link between pairs of two-digit numbers which total 100, for example 37 and 63, and decimals which total 10, such as 3·7 and 6·3. Use a 100-point number line (marked in tens) to model the pairs. The game could be played individually by simply matching the pairs and checking the answers on a calculator.

**Developing Numeracy
Calculations Year 5
© A & C Black**

Game points

- **Write how many more points you need to win each game.**

Draw jumps on the number line to help you count from the smaller number to the larger.

1.

to win:	608 pts
scored:	389 pts
needed:	219 pts

389 → 400 (11) → 600 (200) → 608 (8)

2.

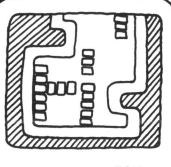

to win:	507 pts
scored:	193 pts
needed:	_____ pts

3.

1300

to win:	712 pts
scored:	486 pts
needed:	_____ pts

4.

4 ooooooo ×3

to win:	6005 pts
scored:	1992 pts
needed:	_____ pts

5.

to win:	8007 pts
scored:	3991 pts
needed:	_____ pts

6.

score 22

to win:	7014 pts
scored:	2986 pts
needed:	_____ pts

Now try this!

- **Write the difference between** 478 **and**

| 607 | _____ | 813 | _____ | 1005 | _____ | 7016 | _____ |

Teachers' note Emphasise that the jumps are best made to the nearest multiple of 100 after the smaller number and the nearest multiple of 100 before the larger. Children may use different 'jumps', for example, to find the difference between 486 and 712 some will jump to 490, then 500, then 700, then 712; others may use only two jumps. Encourage them to use as few jumps as they can.

Developing Numeracy Calculations Year 5 © A & C Black

Dice game

Dice 1

| 235 | 324 | 436 | 143 | 517 | 618 |

Dice 2

| 47 | 58 | 33 | 18 | 26 | 39 |

• **Play this game with a partner.**

☆ Take turns to throw two dice. Find the two matching numbers and add them.

☆ Your partner should check your answer on a calculator.

☆ If the answer is correct and it appears on the board, cover it with a counter.

☆ The winner is the first to get four counters in a row.

You need:
• two dice
• counters in two different colours
• a calculator

When you add, try starting with the hundreds and tens, then add the units.

454	253	556	190	665	363
676	371	564	483	268	182
350	575	282	651	176	382
201	293	475	357	543	469
657	535	494	161	261	636
274	169	342	644	550	462

Teachers' note Use place-value cards to illustrate the partitioning method, for example 235 can be split into 200, 30 and 5; and 47 can be split into 40 and 7. The children can check whether all 36 possible answers exist in the grid by adding each first dice number to each second dice number.

**Developing Numeracy
Calculations Year 5
© A & C Black**

A weighty problem

- **For each question, write the** [total] **weight of the bags.**

1.
1·5 kg
1·6 kg

total ___3·1___ kg

2.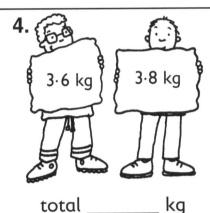
2·6 kg
2·7 kg

total _____ kg

3.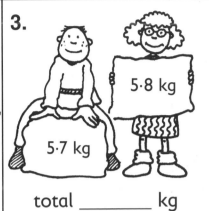
5·8 kg
5·7 kg

total _____ kg

4.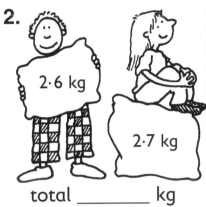
3·6 kg
3·8 kg

total _____ kg

5.
6·8 kg
7·0 kg

total _____ kg

6.
5·5 kg
5·7 kg

total _____ kg

7.
4·5 kg
4·7 kg

total _____ kg

8.
7·6 kg
7·8 kg

total _____ kg

9.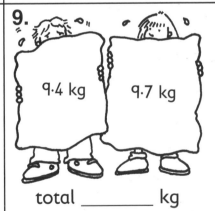
9·4 kg
9·7 kg

total _____ kg

- **Calculate the weight of each bag.**

Now try this!

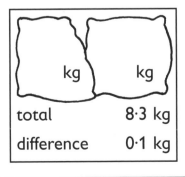
___ kg   ___ kg

total   8·3 kg

difference   0·1 kg

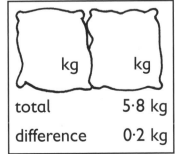
___ kg   ___ kg

total   5·8 kg

difference   0·2 kg

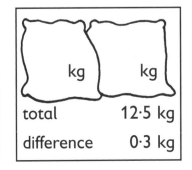
___ kg   ___ kg

total   12·5 kg

difference   0·3 kg

Teachers' note Encourage the children to recognise that when adding 'near doubles' by doubling and adjusting, different methods are possible: for example, ways of adding 5·7 and 5·9 include doubling 5·7 and adjusting by adding 0·2; doubling 5·9 and adjusting by subtracting 0·2; or doubling the mean, i.e. 5·8. Encourage the use of the terms 'doubling' and 'halving'.

**Developing Numeracy
Calculations Year 5
© A & C Black**

TV totals

• Write the **total** cost of the TV and the video recorder.

Add a near multiple of 10 first.

1.
TV £337
recorder £81
total £ _4|8_

2.
TV £156
recorder £79
total £____

3.
TV £423
recorder £76
total £____

4.
TV £357
recorder £72
total £____

5.
TV £413
recorder £69
total £____

6.
TV £534
recorder £88
total £____

• Write the cost of the TV.

Subtract a near multiple of 10 first.

7.
total £483
recorder £61
TV £____

8.
total £417
recorder £78
TV £____

9.
total £285
recorder £72
TV £____

10.
total £496
recorder £83
TV £____

A TV and a video recorder **cost** £284 altogether.

The TV costs three times as much as the recorder.

• How much do they each cost?

TV £ _____   recorder £ _____

Teachers' note Allow the children plenty of practice in doing these calculations mentally, and at speed. Give them confidence to appreciate that adding 69 is no more difficult than adding 71.

**Developing Numeracy
Calculations Year 5
© A & C Black**

Cinema calculations

• **Use the cinema screen to help you find the missing numbers.**

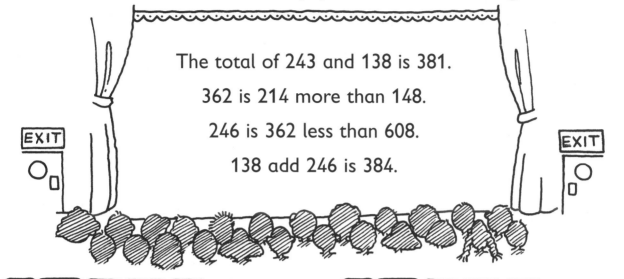

The total of 243 and 138 is 381.

362 is 214 more than 148.

246 is 362 less than 608.

138 add 246 is 384.

1. _____ + 138 = 381

2. _____ + 246 = _____

3. 214 + _____ = _____

4. _____ + 362 = _____

5. _____ − 243 = _____

6. _____ − 138 = _____

7. _____ − 214 = _____

8. _____ − _____ = 362

9. _____ − _____ = 243

10. 384 − _____ = _____

11. 362 − _____ = _____

12. _____ − _____ = 246

• **Write six addition and subtraction sentences using these numbers only.**

213   345   558   96   309

_____   _____   _____

_____   _____   _____

Teachers' note Ensure that the children know how to create three further addition/subtraction facts from one given fact and show them how to check their answers, for example, 381 − 138 = 243 can be checked by adding 243 and 138.

**Developing Numeracy
Calculations Year 5
© A & C Black**

Wordscores

This code gives a value to each letter.

a	b	c	d	e	f	g	h	i	j	k	l	m
9	4	8	4	9	7	6	5	8	2	4	2	3

n	o	p	q	r	s	t	u	v	w	x	y	z
3	7	5	3	5	7	6	7	6	11	1	7	1

• **Add the value for each letter
to calculate these wordscores.**

blue   4 + 2 + 7 + 9 = 22   red _____

green _____   pink _____

grey _____   orange _____

yellow _____   white _____

black _____   purple _____

• **Name each shape. Write its wordscore.**

_____   _____   _____

_____   _____   _____

• **Find three words which have scores
between 20 and 30.**
• **Write the word first and its score beneath.**

_____   _____   _____

_____   _____   _____

Teachers' note Invite the children to discuss different strategies they could use to add the scores, for example, pairing numbers to 10, saving the small numbers to last. As a further extension, ask them to write the score for the longest word they can think of.

**Developing Numeracy
Calculations Year 5
© A & C Black**

L-shapes

The L-shapes all come from this grid.

• Write the numbers in each shape to show where it comes from.

90	30	40	60	80
20	80	70	50	60
80	40	90	60	90
40	30	90	20	50
50	60	70	70	80

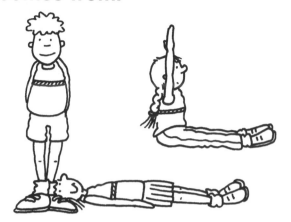

1.

40	60
70	

total 170

2.

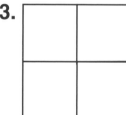

total 160

3.

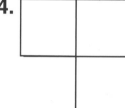

total 140

4.

total 200

5.

total 200

6.

total 190

7.

total 180

8.

total 110

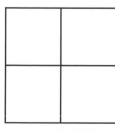

• **Find these squares in the grid.**

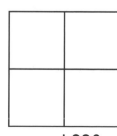

total 280

total 220

Teachers' note Encourage the children to make the links between adding multiples of ten, for example 80, 70 and 40, and adding single digits, such as 8, 7 and 4 (adding 80, 70 and 40 is equivalent to adding 8, 7 and 4 tens). There are several possible solutions to some of the questions on this page.

**Developing Numeracy
Calculations Year 5
© A & C Black**

Clover leaves

- **Write the** total **for each three-leaf clover.**

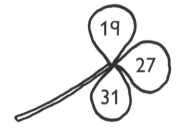

 Look for pairs which make a multiple of 10, and add these first.

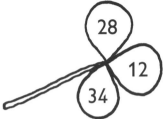

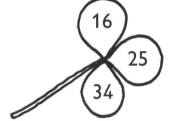

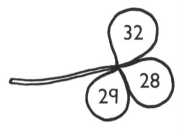

28 12 34

16 25 34

19 27 31

1. total _74_

2. total _____

3. total _____

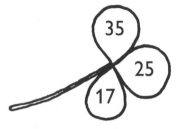

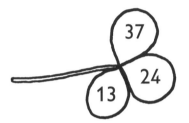

35 25 17

37 24 13

32 28 29

4. total _____

5. total _____

6. total _____

- **Use the same method to find the total for each four-leaf clover.**

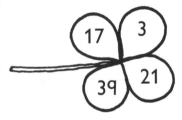

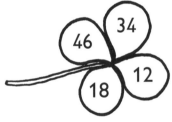

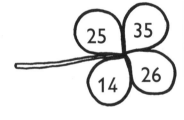

17 3 39 21

46 34 18 12

25 35 14 26

7. total _____

8. total _____

9. total _____

 Now try this!

- **Write four different numbers which have these totals.**

Make pairs whose units digits total 10.

total 100   total 120

Teachers' note When adding 28, 34 and 12 the children can choose to look for numbers which make multiples of 10, for example 28 and 12, add these together first (40), then add the other number. Alternatively they can start by adding the tens (60), then add on the units looking for pairs which make 10 (8 + 2).

**Developing Numeracy
Calculations Year 5
© A & C Black**

16

Don't be shy!

• Find each total by multiplying.

1.

total __3__ x __15__ = __45__

2.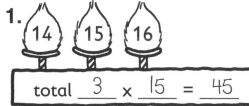

total __3__ x ____ = ____

3.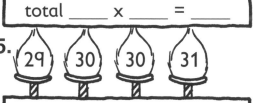

total ____ x ____ = ____

4.

total ____ x ____ = ____

5.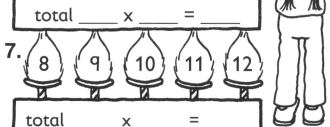

total ____ x ____ = ____

6.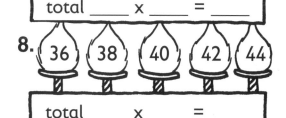

total ____ x ____ = ____

7.

total ____ x ____ = ____

8.

total ____ x ____ = ____

• Write the missing numbers.

9. 8 10

total 30

10. 50 53

total 150

11. 16 20 20

total 80

12. 27 30 33

total 120

13. 37 40 43

total 200

14. 26 28 32

total 150

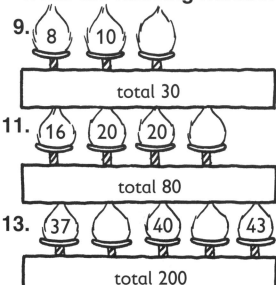

• **Write different sets of five numbers. Each set must have a total of** 150 .

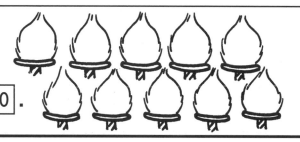

Teachers' note Some children may need to write a middle step, for example 14 + 15 + 16 = 15 + 15 + 15. They may need this modelled practically. The activity can be extended to using the same strategy to add a set of numbers which are nearly a multiple, then adjusting: for example, to add 29, 31, 32, 36 calculate 4 x 30, then add 2 and 6.

**Developing Numeracy
Calculations Year 5
© A & C Black**

Movie maths

- **Write how many people are watching each film.**

children 240, adults 470

total 710

children 350, adults 260

total _____

children 430, adults 490

total _____

children 230, adults 180

total _____

children 460, adults 150

total _____

children 370, adults 350

total _____

- **Write how many <u>children</u> are watching each film.**

total   370

adults   180

children _____

total   520

adults   190

children _____

total   440

adults   270

children _____

- ☐ 630 people ☐ **are watching a film. There are** ☐ 70 ☐ **more adults than children. Write how many of each.**

adults _____   children _____

The tickets cost ☐ £5 ☐ **each.**

- **How much money was paid?** _____

Teachers' note Encourage the children to recognise that the calculations are equivalent to adding a pair of two-digit numbers, and to use similar strategies. In the plenary session, the children could explain the methods they used to do the calculations. As a further extension, ask them to calculate the money taken at the box office, giving them an appropriate price for adult/child tickets.

Developing Numeracy
Calculations Year 5
© A & C Black

Rows and columns

• Write the total for each row and each column.

300	200	400	900
100	500	600	____
800	700	900	____

1200 ____ ____

400	700	600	400	____
500	300	500	100	____
700	400	200	600	____
300	200	500	300	____

____ ____ ____ ____

• Write the missing numbers.

900	700		1900
	100	600	900
500		400	1700

____ ____ ____

100		200	____
	500	400	____
400	300		____

800 1600 800

All rows, columns **and** diagonals have a total of ⟨1500⟩.

• Fill in the missing numbers.

	100	
400		200

Teachers' note Encourage the children to recognise that the calculations are equivalent to adding several one-digit numbers, and to use similar strategies.

**Developing Numeracy
Calculations Year 5
© A & C Black**

Jaws!

• **Play this game with a partner.**

☆ Cut out the two sets of cards.

☆ Shuffle each set. Place them face
   down in two separate piles.

☆ Take turns to pick a card from each
   pile. Subtract the smaller number from
   the larger.

☆ If you are correct, score points to match
   the hundreds digit of the answer (for
   example, score 4 if the answer is 465).

☆ Have ten rounds each, reshuffling the
   cards when necessary.

Name	Name
Score	**Score**

Round 1		
Round 2		
Round 3		

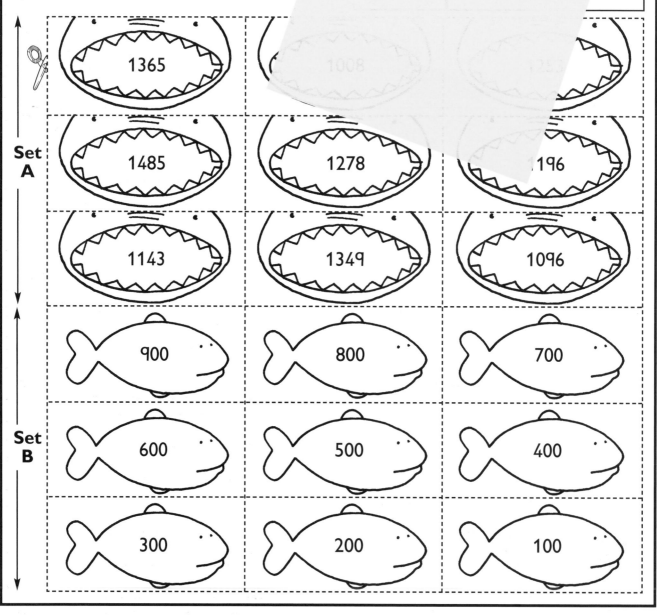

Set A

1365	1008	
1485	1278	1196
1143	1349	1096

Set B

900	800	700
600	500	400
300	200	100

Teachers' note Photocopy the game onto card and laminate to make a reusable resource. The
children should check each other's answers, using a calculator if necessary. After ten rounds, they
can each total their points to find the winner. A variation of the game can be played, where the children
add the two card numbers instead of subtracting.

**Developing Numeracy
Calculations Year 5
© A & C Black**

Home and Away

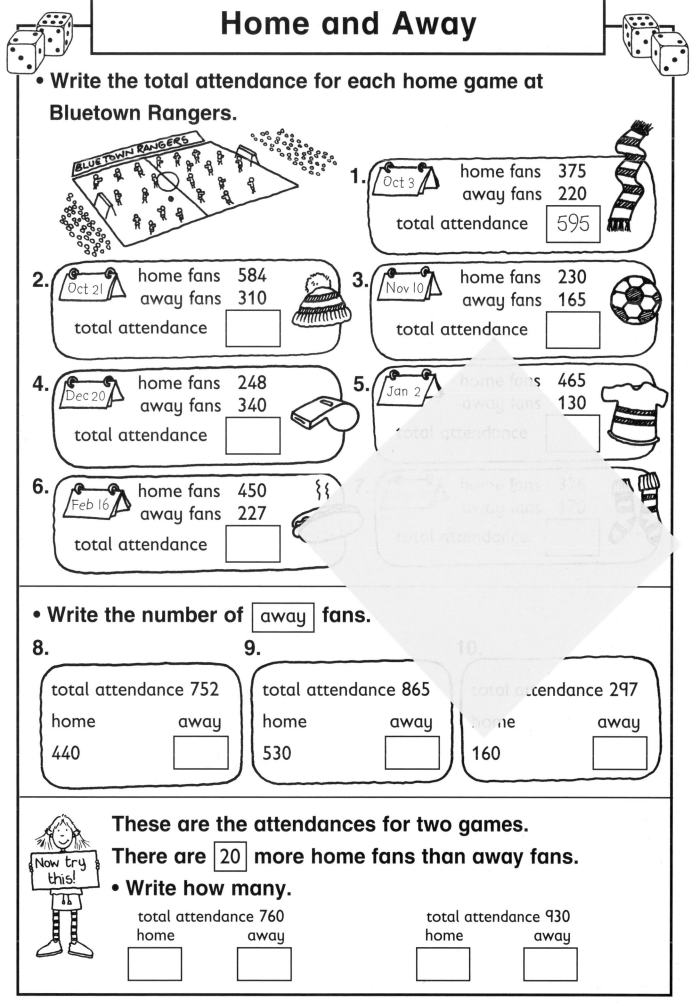

- **Write the total attendance for each home game at Bluetown Rangers.**

1. Oct 3
home fans 375
away fans 220
total attendance 595

2. Oct 21
home fans 584
away fans 310
total attendance

3. Nov 10
home fans 230
away fans 165
total attendance

4. Dec 20
home fans 248
away fans 340
total attendance

5. Jan 2
home fans 465
away fans 130
total attendance

6. Feb 16
home fans 450
away fans 227
total attendance

7. home fans 375
away fans 170
total attendance

- **Write the number of** away **fans.**

8. total attendance 752
home 440   away

9. total attendance 865
home 530   away

10. total attendance 297
home 160   away

These are the attendances for two games.

There are 20 more home fans than away fans.

- **Write how many.**

total attendance 760
home   away

total attendance 930
home   away

Now try this!

Teachers' note Encourage the children to develop a systematic method for adding larger numbers, for example, for 474 + 320 first add 300, then 20 (followed by the units if there are any).

**Developing Numeracy
Calculations Year 5
© A & C Black**

Mouse or Mighty

The target is to reach the next hundred marker.

• **Write how many more points each person needs.**

1.

734 + __66__ = __800__

2.

463 + _____ = _____

3.

275 + _____ = _____

4.

583 + _____ = _____

5.

369 + _____ = _____

6.

838 + _____ = _____

• **Write how many points have been scored.**

7. 47 needed to reach 800.
scored _____

8. 68 needed to reach 400.
scored _____

9.  73 needed to reach 500.
scored _____

 Now try this!

Khalid needs 52 to reach 700.
score _____

Jill needs 17 to reach 600.
score _____

Lee needs 79 to reach 800.
score _____

• **Write the difference in points between:**

Khalid and Lee _____

Khalid and Jill _____

Jill and Lee _____

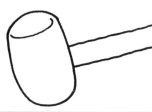

Teachers' note The amount to add can be modelled using a 100-point unmarked number line: for example, to find what to add to 734, assume that the line shows 700 to 800. Locate 734 on the line and show the distance to 800 as six tens and six units.

**Developing Numeracy
Calculations Year 5
© A & C Black**

Hive of activity

This is a game for two or three players.

You need:
- a dice marked 0·1 to 0·6
- a counter each in different colours

☆ Place your counter on a bee.
☆ Take turns to throw the dice. Move your counter to a touching number if, when added to the dice number, it makes a **whole** number. Otherwise stay where you are.
☆ The winner is the first to reach a flower.

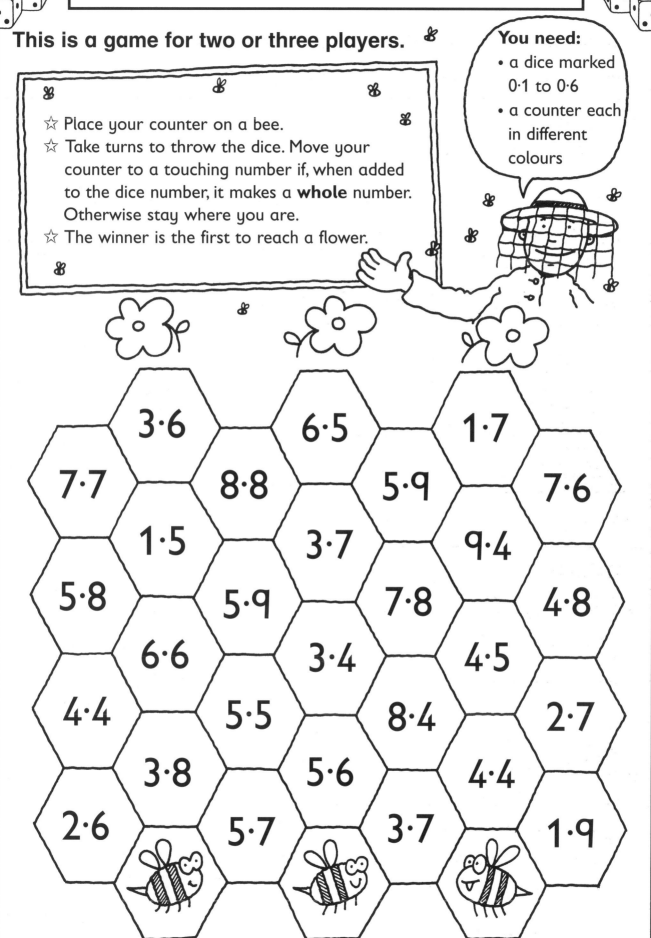

Teachers' note Encourage the children to recognise that three skills involved are the same as for adding a one-digit number to make the next multiple of 10. They could play the game individually by writing the dice score beside the matching number and checking the answers on a calculator at the end.

Developing Numeracy
Calculations Year 5
© A & C Black

Discount Dan

- **Write how much** | discount | **(money taken off the price)**
  for each car.

DAN'S discount deals

1.
old price £5009
sale price £4987
discount £ _22_

2.
old price £6002
sale price £5899
discount £_____

3.
old price £7009
sale price £6972
discount £_____

4.
old price £8001
sale price £7888
discount £_____

5.
old price £4007
sale price £3895
discount £_____

- **Write the sale prices for these cars.**

6.
old price £7001
discount £ 104
sale price £_____

7.
old price £4005
discount £ 109
sale price £_____

8.
old price £6011
discount £ 116
sale price £_____

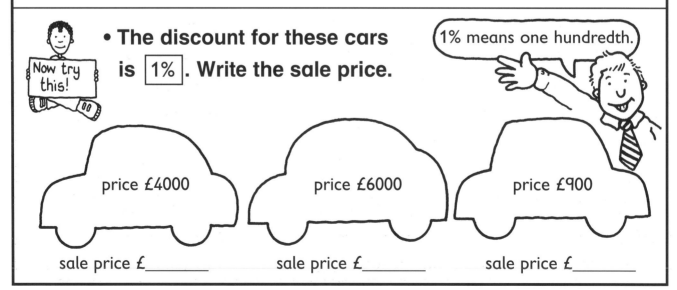

Now try this!

- **The discount for these cars**
  is | 1% |. **Write the sale price.**

1% means one hundredth.

price £4000

price £6000

price £900

sale price £_____

sale price £_____

sale price £_____

Teachers' note The children can draw a number line to 'make a picture' of the jumps needed to
count from the smaller number to the larger. Encourage them not to count on in ones, but to use their
knowledge of number facts to count on in larger jumps, bridging to the multiple of 1000.

**Developing Numeracy
Calculations Year 5
© A & C Black**

Wizards

The wizards are making their noses grow longer !

• Write the new length.

1.

4·8 cm

3·5 cm longer
new length __8·3__ cm

2.

2·9 cm

1·2 cm longer
new length _____ cm

3.

3·6 cm

1·7 cm longer
new length _____ cm

4.

6·4 cm

2·9 cm longer
new length _____ cm

5.
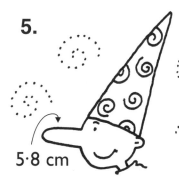

5·8 cm

3·6 cm longer
new length _____ cm

6.
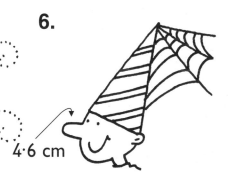

4·6 cm

1·7 cm longer
new length _____ cm

Each wizard cuts his or her nails shorter by magic!

• Write the new length.

7.   5·1 cm
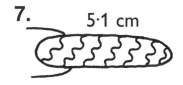

1·4 cm shorter
new length _____ cm

8.   7·5 cm

1·8 cm shorter
new length _____ cm

9.   8·3 cm
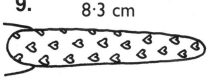

2·7 cm shorter
new length _____ cm

10.   5·4 cm

1·8 cm shorter
new length _____ cm

11.   9·2 cm
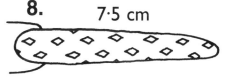

4·5 cm shorter
new length _____ cm

12.   6·3 cm
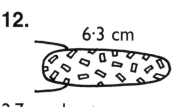

2·7 cm shorter
new length _____ cm

Teachers' note The additions can be modelled using a 100-point unmarked number line with the ends labelled 0 and 10. As an extension, the children can make up more 'nose' or 'nail' problems for a partner to solve.

**Developing Numeracy
Calculations Year 5
© A & C Black**

Addition countdown

Addition Countdown

- **Write an estimate for each addition.**
- **Complete the additions.**
- **Write the difference between the answer and your estimate.**

Start with thousands, then hundreds, then tens, then units.

	Estimate	Answer	Difference
1			
2			
3			
4			
5			

1.
```
  2 8 7 1
+ 4 3 2 6
---------
  6 0 0 0
  1 1 0 0
      9 0
        7
---------

```

2.
```
  3 7 4 6
+ 1 5 4 9
---------


```

3.
```
  4 2 8 9
+ 3 7 3 5
---------


```

4.
```
  5 0 9 4
+ 1 8 6 7
---------


```

5.
```
  3 2 8 5
+ 4 9 6 7
---------


```

- **Ring your best estimate.**

Now try this!

- **Write an estimate for this addition.**

  estimate [＿＿＿＿＿]

- **Then find the answer.**

```
  5 7 7 2
  7 2 5 6
+ 2 8 7 5
---------


```

Teachers' note Remind the children how to round a four-digit number to the nearest 1000 before they begin the activity. This can be used to help their estimates. Some children may be confident enough to give a more accurate estimate by rounding to the nearest 100. They may enjoy doing the activity against the clock.

**Developing Numeracy
Calculations Year 5
© A & C Black**

Wrestle to 1000

• **Play this game with a partner.**

You need a dice.

☆ Each player writes their name at the top of a strip.

☆ Roll a dice. Both players write that number in any one of their boxes.

☆ Do this six times until each player has created two 3-digit numbers. Add your numbers together.

☆ Calculate the **difference** between your answer and 1000. This is your score.

☆ The player with the **lowest** score wins the round.

Example:

	4	3	6
+	2	5	3
	6	8	9

Score 3 1 1

Name _____

Round **1**

```
  ┌──┬──┬──┐
  │  │  │  │
  ├──┼──┼──┤
+ │  │  │  │
  └──┴──┴──┘
  _____
```

Score _____

Round **2**

Score _____

Round **3**

Score _____

Name _____

Round **1**

Score _____

Round **2**

Score _____

Round **3**

Score _____

Teachers' note Variations of the game can be played with a different target figure, such as 1200 or 700. Alternatively, the children can aim to make the largest or smallest possible total; in this case the player with the larger/smaller total scores zero and the other player scores the difference between their two totals.

**Developing Numeracy
Calculations Year 5
© A & C Black**

A sticky situation

Josh has stuck sticky stars on his big sister's homework!

• **Calculate the hidden numbers.**

1.
```
  ☆ 3 2 5
+ 2 ☆ 6 4
─────────
  6 4 ☆ 9
```

2.
```
  3 7 ☆ 2
+ ☆ 4 6 ☆
─────────
  8 2 1 7
    1 1
```

3.
```
  ☆ 8 6 2
+ 3 7 1 5
─────────
  8 ☆ ☆ 7
    1
```

4.
```
  ☆ 9 3 ☆
+ 4 2 ☆ 1
─────────
  7 ☆ 0 9
    1 1
```

5.
```
  2 ☆ 6 3
+ 3 5 ☆ 8
─────────
  ☆ 1 8 ☆
  1     1
```

6.
```
  4 ☆ 9 ☆
+ 1 9 ☆ 6
─────────
  ☆ 7 2 8
  1   1
```

7.
```
  5 ☆ 4 3
+ ☆ 1 ☆ 9
─────────
  8 0 1 ☆
  1 1 1
```

8.
```
  4 ☆ 8 ☆
+ 4 6 7 3
─────────
  ☆ 0 ☆ 8
  1   1
```

9.
```
  2 ☆ 9 ☆
+ 1 3 ☆ 9
─────────
  ☆ 9 8 3
  1     1
```

• **Write additions which have these answers.**

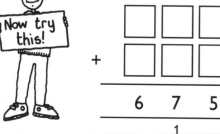

Now try this!

```
  □ □ □
+ □ □ □
─────────
6 7 5 2
    1
```

```
  □ □ □ □
+ □ □ □
─────────
9 4 6 3
  1 1
```

Teachers' note Some children may benefit from using base 10 material on a place-value board to help model the missing number problems. The children can check their answers with a calculator. As a further extension, they could find two different additions for the answers in the extension.

**Developing Numeracy
Calculations Year 5
© A & C Black**

Wrestle to 100

• Play this game with a partner.

You need a dice.

☆ Each player writes their name at the top of a strip.

☆ Roll a dice. Both players write that number in any one of their boxes.

☆ Do this six times until each player has created two 3-digit decimal numbers. Add <u>your</u> numbers together.

☆ Calculate the **difference** between your answer and 100. This is your score.

☆ The player with the **lowest** score wins the round.

Example:

	4	3	.	6
+	2	5	.	3
	6	8	.	9

Score 3 1 · 1

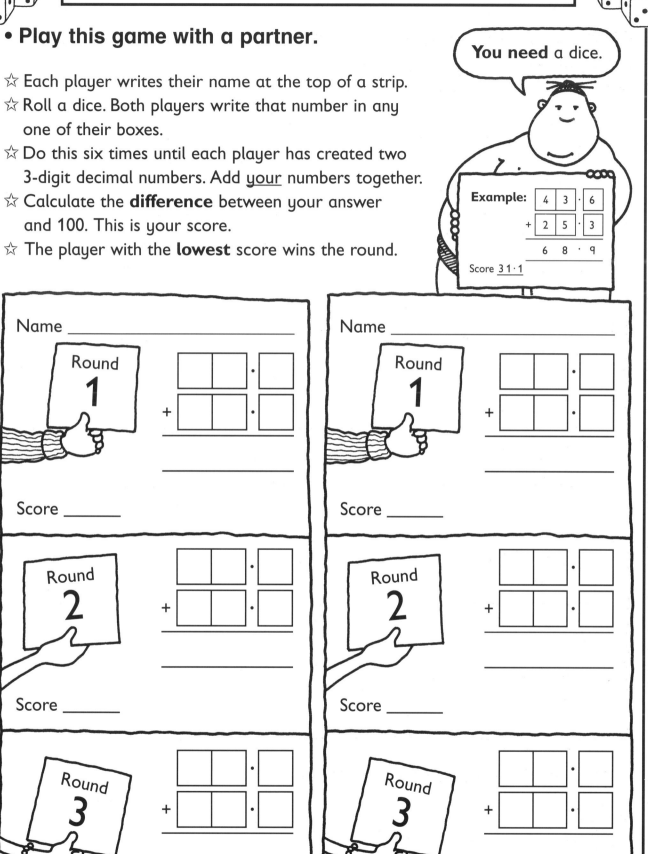

Name _____

Round **1**

Score _____

Round **2**

Score _____

Round **3**

Score _____

Name _____

Round **1**

Score _____

Round **2**

Score _____

Round **3**

Score _____

Teachers' note Encourage the children to talk through the calculations, referring to the digits in terms of tens, units or tenths: for example, 'Seven tenths and six tenths is thirteen tenths, which is one unit and three tenths.'

**Developing Numeracy
Calculations Year 5
© A & C Black**

Caravan holidays

These families are travelling abroad with their caravans.

• Write how many miles each family still has to go.

1.

643 mile journey. 185 miles travelled so far.

```
  6 4 3
-  1 8 5
    1 5  makes 200
  4 0 0  makes 600
    4 3  makes 643
    4 5 8
```

2.

538 mile journey. 279 miles travelled so far.

−

3.

823 mile journey. 569 miles travelled so far.

−

4.

734 mile journey. 189 miles travelled so far.

−

5.

951 mile journey. 466 miles travelled so far.

−

6.

437 mile journey. 279 miles travelled so far.

−

Now try this!

• **Find the difference between the largest and smallest answers you calculated.**

−

Teachers' note This recording method mirrors the use of a number line as a visual representation of counting from the smaller number to the larger. Some children may find it helpful to draw hops on a blank number line. If you do not wish to prescribe a method, mask out the worked example. Children can check their answers by adding the answer to the smaller number (it should make the larger number).

Developing Numeracy Calculations Year 5 © A & C Black

Book at bedtime

• **Calculate how many pages are left to read.**

1.

189 pages read out of 543.

$$543 = 500 + 40 + 3$$
$$-189 \qquad 100 + 80 + 9$$
$$\overline{354}$$
$$= 500 + 30 + 13$$
$$\qquad 100 + 80 + 9$$

$$= 400 + 130 + 13$$
$$\qquad 100 + 80 + 9$$
$$\overline{300 + 50 + 4}$$

2.

275 pages read out of 632.

$$632$$
$$-275$$
$$\overline{}$$

3.

377 pages read out of 944.

4.

386 pages read out of 855.

5.

158 pages read out of 672.

6.

279 pages read out of 513.

Teachers' note This method can be clearly demonstrated using base 10 material on a place-value board (or using an OHP and base 10 material constructed for use on an OHP). If you do not wish to prescribe a method, mask out the worked example before giving the sheet to the children. As an extension, the children can make up their own 'book' problems for a partner to solve.

Developing Numeracy Calculations Year 5 © A & C Black

Be the teacher!

- Mark Ruby's homework. ☑ or ☒
- Ring any errors.
- Give a mark out of 12.

1.
```
   7 1
6 8̷ 1
- 1 3 5
─────────
④ 4 6  ✗
```

2.
```
  4 1
5̷ 3 8
- 3 4 6
─────────
  1 9 2
```

3.
```
  7 1
7 8̷ 3
- 2 4 6
─────────
  5 3 7
```

4.
```
  4 1
2 5̷ 7
- 1 3 9
─────────
  1 1 8
```

5.
```
  8 1
9̷ 1 3
- 4 8 2
─────────
  4 2 1
```

6.
```
  3 1
4̷ 3 6
- 1 8 3
─────────
  2 5 3
```

7.
```
  5 1
5 4̷ 1
- 1 2 9
─────────
  4 3 2
```

8.
```
  3 11 1
4 2̷ 3
- 3 4 5
─────────
    7 8
```

9.
```
  4 14 1
3̷ 5̷ 2
- 1 6 6
─────────
  3 8 6
```

10.
```
  4 10 1
5̷ 1̷ 4
- 1 9 7
─────────
  3 1 7
```

11.
```
  3 12 1
4̷ 3̷ 2
- 2 8 6
─────────
  1 3 6
```

12.
```
  5 1
6̷ 2 7
- 3 7 4
─────────
  2 5 3
```

mark /12

- Estimate which of these subtractions will have an answer closer to ☐300☐. Tick ☐A☐ or ☐B☐.
- Now subtract them to see if you were correct.

A
```
  7 1 4
- 3 9 3
─────────
```

B
```
  5 1 8
- 2 3 1
─────────
```

Teachers' note The method of decomposition can be clearly demonstrated using base 10 material on a place-value board (or using an OHP and base 10 material constructed for use on an OHP). This more sophisticated recording method follows from the expanded form used on the previous sheet. The children can be asked to rewrite correctly the incorrect subtractions.

**Developing Numeracy
Calculations Year 5
© A & C Black**

Shape name puzzle

- **For each subtraction, estimate first, then subtract.**

S

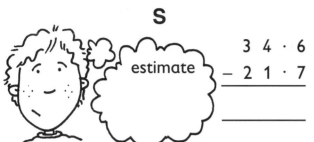

estimate

$$
\begin{array}{r}
3\ 4\ \cdot\ 6 \\
-\ 2\ 1\ \cdot\ 7 \\
\hline
\end{array}
$$

H

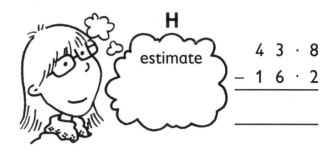

estimate

$$
\begin{array}{r}
4\ 3\ \cdot\ 8 \\
-\ 1\ 6\ \cdot\ 2 \\
\hline
\end{array}
$$

E

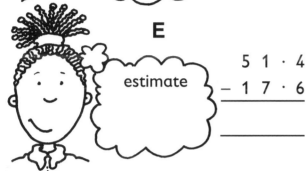

estimate

$$
\begin{array}{r}
5\ 1\ \cdot\ 4 \\
-\ 1\ 7\ \cdot\ 6 \\
\hline
\end{array}
$$

R

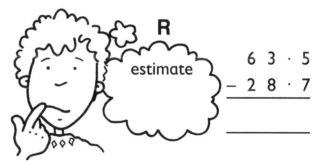

estimate

$$
\begin{array}{r}
6\ 3\ \cdot\ 5 \\
-\ 2\ 8\ \cdot\ 7 \\
\hline
\end{array}
$$

E

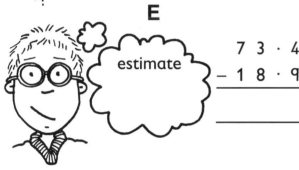

estimate

$$
\begin{array}{r}
7\ 3\ \cdot\ 4 \\
-\ 1\ 8\ \cdot\ 9 \\
\hline
\end{array}
$$

P

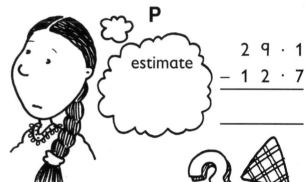

estimate

$$
\begin{array}{r}
2\ 9\ \cdot\ 1 \\
-\ 1\ 2\ \cdot\ 7 \\
\hline
\end{array}
$$

- **Now write the letters in order (smallest to largest answer) to spell a shape name.**

_____ _____ _____ _____ _____ _____

Now try this!

- **Use the six answers above to complete these subtractions.**

$$
\begin{array}{r}
\square\ \square\ \cdot\ \square \\
-\ \square\ \square\ \cdot\ \square \\
\hline
2\ 6\ \cdot\ 9
\end{array}
\qquad
\begin{array}{r}
\square\ \square\ \cdot\ \square \\
-\ \square\ \square\ \cdot\ \square \\
\hline
2\ 0\ \cdot\ 9
\end{array}
\qquad
\begin{array}{r}
\square\ \square\ \cdot\ \square \\
-\ \square\ \square\ \cdot\ \square \\
\hline
1\ 8\ \cdot\ 4
\end{array}
$$

Teachers' note Before beginning the activity, let the children practise their rounding skills. It is sufficient to round the whole number parts to their nearest 10, then subtract to achieve an estimate. Some children may feel confident enough to give a more accurate estimate by rounding to the nearest whole number.

**Developing Numeracy
Calculations Year 5
© A & C Black**

Bracket brainteaser

- **Cut out the cards. Use them to complete the calculations.**

You can use each digit only once in each calculation.

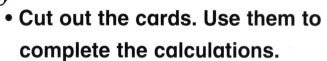

1.
$$(\underline{\quad} + \underline{\quad}) \times \underline{\quad} = 16$$

2.
$$(\underline{\quad} \times \underline{\quad}) + \underline{\quad} = 32$$

3.
$$(\underline{\quad} + \underline{\quad}) \times \underline{\quad} = 33$$

4.
$$(\underline{\quad} \times \underline{\quad}) - \underline{\quad} = 13$$

5.
$$\underline{\quad} + (\underline{\quad} \times \underline{\quad}) = 12$$

6.
$$\underline{\quad} + (\underline{\quad} \times \underline{\quad}) = 23$$

7.
$$(\underline{\quad} \times \underline{\quad}) + (\underline{\quad} \times \underline{\quad}) = 36$$

8.
$$(\underline{\quad} + \underline{\quad}) \times \underline{\quad} = 42$$

9.
$$(\underline{\quad} \times \underline{\quad}) - \underline{\quad} = 9$$

10.
$$(\underline{\quad} + \underline{\quad} + \underline{\quad}) \times \underline{\quad} = 60$$

Now try this!

- **Use the cards to help you write calculations with these totals.**

Use brackets.

(18) (20) (19) (14) (3)

(	)	2	3	5	6	x
(	)	+	+	–	–	x

Teachers' note Give the children examples to demonstrate the need for brackets, for example, show that (3 + 5) x 2 and 3 + (5 x 2) produce different answers.

Developing Numeracy Calculations Year 5
© A & C Black

Cracker packer

This machine packs crackers in boxes.

- Write how many boxes will be full.
- Write the remainder as a ⌈fraction⌉.

1.

46 crackers
boxes of 5

$\underline{46} \div \underline{5} = \underline{9\frac{1}{5}}$

2.

35 crackers
boxes of 6

_____ ÷ _____ = _____

3.

28 crackers
boxes of 3

_____ ÷ _____ = _____

4.

24 crackers
boxes of 7

_____ ÷ _____ = _____

5.

43 crackers
boxes of 8

_____ ÷ _____ = _____

6.

29 crackers
boxes of 4

_____ ÷ _____ = _____

- **Write how many crackers there are in total.**

7.
boxes of 5
$4\frac{3}{5}$ boxes

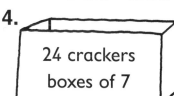

23 crackers

8.
boxes of 7
$5\frac{2}{7}$ boxes

crackers

9.
boxes of 4
$3\frac{3}{4}$ boxes

crackers

10.
boxes of 9
$2\frac{7}{9}$ boxes

crackers

11.
boxes of 8
$1\frac{5}{8}$ boxes

crackers

12.
boxes of 6
$5\frac{5}{6}$ boxes

crackers

Teachers' note The divisions can be modelled using interlocking cubes: for example, read 46 ÷ 5 as 'forty-six divided by five', as well as 'how many fives make forty-six?' The children can make towers of five, which will show the remainder of one as a fifth of a tower.

**Developing Numeracy
Calculations Year 5
© A & C Black**

Money go round

• **Play this game with a partner.**

You need:
• a counter each
• a large pile of 1p coins
• a dice

$36 \div 4$ $\frac{1}{3}$ of 15 $\frac{1}{3}$ of 24

$\frac{40}{10}$ $21 \div 3$

$\frac{1}{10}$ of 20 $23 \div 4$

$\frac{16}{3}$ $\frac{18}{3}$

$27 \div 3$ $\frac{1}{4}$ of 24

☆ Place your counter on any square.
☆ Take turns to throw a dice and move your counter.
☆ Say the answer to the division you land on. If there is a remainder, say it as a **fraction**.
☆ If your partner agrees, collect 1p coins to match the whole number part of the answer.
☆ The first to collect 50p wins the game.

$\frac{1}{2}$ of 18 $17 \div 5$

$27 \div 10$ $44 \div 4$

$30 \div 10$ $13 \over 2$

$\frac{12}{2}$ $\frac{28}{4}$

$\frac{1}{5}$ of 20 $14 \div 2$ $\frac{30}{5}$ $35 \div 5$ $\frac{1}{4}$ of 16

Teachers' note Before beginning the activity, remind the children that there are different ways to write a division, for example $\frac{1}{4}$ of 12, $12 \div 4$, $\frac{12}{4}$. To reduce the number of 1p coins needed, the children could exchange ten 1p coins for a 10p coin.

**Developing Numeracy
Calculations Year 5
© A & C Black**

Animal tokens game

- **Play this game with a partner.**

☆ Place a counter on each token.

☆ Take turns to remove a counter. Divide the number revealed
   by 10 and say the answer as a **decimal**.

   Example: 43 ÷ 10 = 4·3 (say 'four point three')

☆ If your partner agrees, keep the counter. If not, replace it.

☆ The winner is the player who collects the most counters.

☆ Now play three more games for ÷ 2 , ÷ 5 and ÷ 4 .

43 61 29 15 24 45

27 64 51 29 19 72

93 38 57 83 9

85 50 91 35 53

Teachers' note This game can also be used to give practice in expressing remainders either as whole
numbers or as fractions. Children can use the sheet individually by recording the division and answer
as each token is uncovered.

**Developing Numeracy
Calculations Year 5**
© A & C Black

Multiplication wheels

• **Multiply each number in the middle ring by the number in the centre. Write the answer in the outer ring.**

1.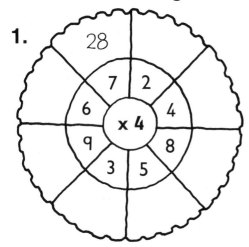

(centre: × 4, middle ring: 7, 2, 6, 4, 9, 8, 3, 5; outer: 28)

2.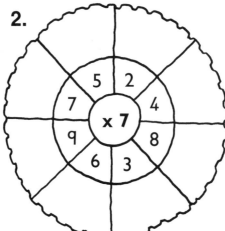

(centre: × 7, middle ring: 5, 2, 7, 4, 9, 8, 6, 3)

• **Write your own numbers on these wheels.**

3.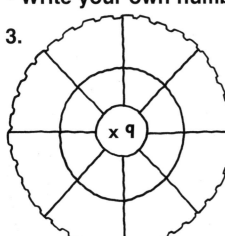

(centre: × 9)

4.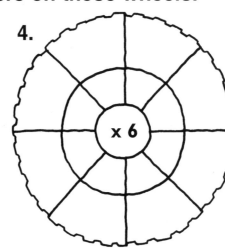

(centre: × 6)

• **Choose your own centre numbers. Complete the wheels.**

Now try this!

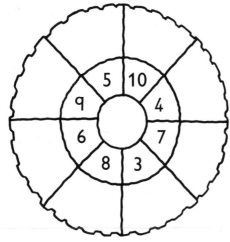

(middle ring: 5, 10, 9, 4, 6, 7, 8, 3)

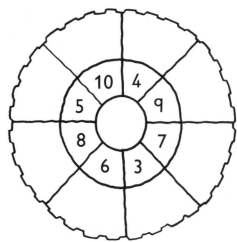

(middle ring: 10, 4, 5, 9, 8, 7, 6, 3)

Teachers' note Some children may have difficulty recalling the facts. Suggest they use known multiplication facts, for example: derive 6 x 8 from 3 x 8 by doubling; derive 9 x 6 from 10 x 6 by subtracting. For the extension activity, ask the children to choose different centre numbers from those on the rest of the page.

**Developing Numeracy
Calculations Year 5
© A & C Black**

Magic carpets

- Write the [area] of each square carpet.

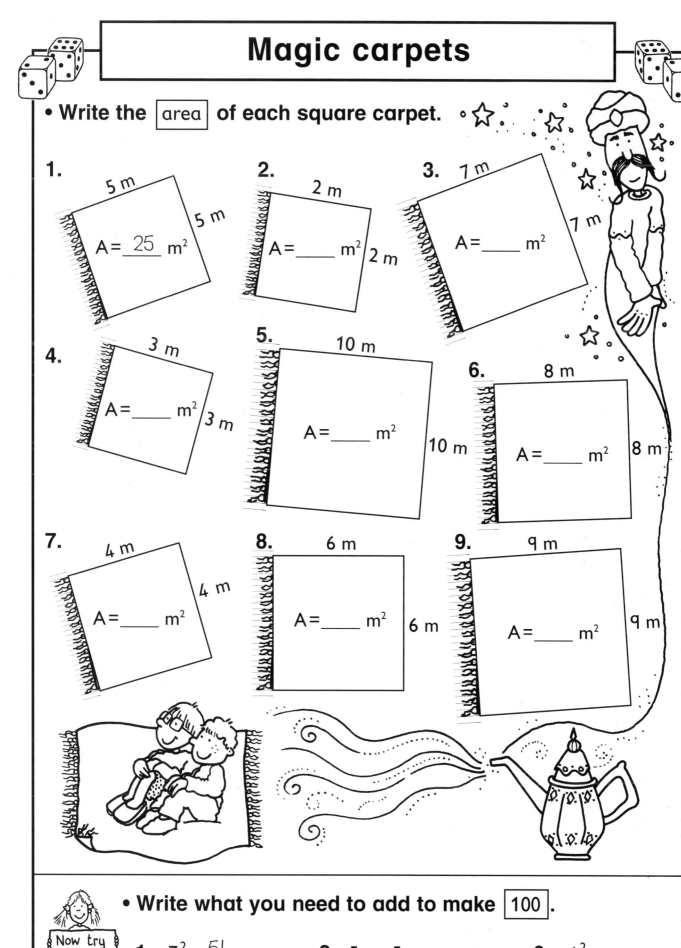

1.
5 m   5 m
A = _25_ m²

2.
2 m   2 m
A = ____ m²

3.
7 m   7 m
A = ____ m²

4.
3 m   3 m
A = ____ m²

5.
10 m   10 m
A = ____ m²

6.
8 m   8 m
A = ____ m²

7.
4 m   4 m
A = ____ m²

8.
6 m   6 m
A = ____ m²

9.
q m   q m
A = ____ m²

Now try this!

- **Write what you need to add to make** [100].

1. 7^2 _51_

2. 5 x 5 ____

3. 6^2 ____

4. q^2 ____

5. 8 x 8 ____

6. 4^2 ____

Teachers' note The children should be encouraged to recall immediately the squares of numbers from 1 to 10. Locate them on the diagonal of a multiplication square and give regular practice in chanting them in sequence. Ensure that the children are familiar with the index notation for square numbers.

**Developing Numeracy
Calculations Year 5**
© A & C Black

• **Play this game with a partner.**

☆ Start at the entrance. Take turns to toss a coin and move your counter. Heads = forward 1   Tails = forward 2

☆ Answer the division where you land. Your partner checks your answer. If you are incorrect, miss your next turn. If the answer is **5**, jump up a row. If it is **4**, move down a row.

☆ The winner is the first to reach the exit.

> **You need** a counter each and a coin.

$36 \div 4$	$32 \div 8$	$72 \div 9$	$42 \div 7$	$42 \div 6$	exit $35 \div 7$
$63 \div 9$	$24 \div 6$	$28 \div 7$	$40 \div 5$	$54 \div 6$	$48 \div 8$
$30 \div 6$	$63 \div 7$	$24 \div 4$	$36 \div 9$	$45 \div 9$	$45 \div 5$
$48 \div 6$	$36 \div 9$	$40 \div 8$	$35 \div 7$	$35 \div 5$	$56 \div 7$
$32 \div 8$	$20 \div 4$	$56 \div 8$	$30 \div 5$	$45 \div 9$	$32 \div 4$
$28 \div 4$	$28 \div 7$	$40 \div 8$	$25 \div 5$	$20 \div 5$	$16 \div 4$
entrance	$81 \div 9$	$54 \div 9$	$36 \div 6$	$49 \div 7$	$72 \div 8$

Teachers' note Encourage the children to relate division facts to multiplication facts, for example, $45 \div 9$ can be read as, 'How many nines make forty-five?', and requires a recall of 9 times table facts.

Developing Numeracy
Calculations Year 5
© A & C Black

Darts doubles

• Write the total score for each pair of darts. The outer ring counts as double .

To double 43, first double 40, then double 3 and add them together.

Board 1

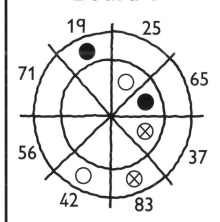

19   25
71   65
56   37
42   83

● and ● ___103___

○ and ○ _____

⊗ and ⊗ _____

Board 2

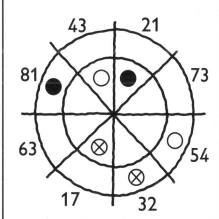

43   21
81   73
63   54
17   32

● and ● _____

○ and ○ _____

⊗ and ⊗ _____

Board 3

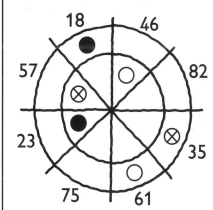

18   46
57   82
23   35
75   61

● and ● _____

○ and ○ _____

⊗ and ⊗ _____

Now try this!

• Write down the numbers on each dartboard which are greater than 50 . Double them.

Board 1

65 ⟶ 130

83 ⟶ _____

56 ⟶ _____

71 ⟶ _____

Board 2

_____

_____

_____

_____

Board 3

_____

_____

_____

_____

• For each board, write the highest score you can get with three darts.

Board 1 _____   Board 2 _____   Board 3 _____

Teachers' note Suggest strategies for finding the doubles of two-digit numbers, for example, for 46: double the tens (80), double the units (12) and combine (92); or double 50 (100), double 4 (8) and subtract (92). The children should do their workings for the main activity on a separate sheet of paper.

Developing Numeracy Calculations Year 5 © A & C Black

Tower Power

- **Play this game with a partner.**

  You need 18 counters.

☆ Place a counter on each spot.

☆ Take turns to remove a counter and say the answer.

☆ Your partner checks your answer. If it appears on the tower, cover it with the counter. If it does not, or if your answer is incorrect, replace the counter.

☆ Score points for each answer you cover.

☆ The game ends when the tower is complete. The winner is the player with the most points.

1440	6 pts
270	3 pts
1660	11 pts
140	1 pt
1860	9 pts
340	5 pts
750	12 pts
410	2 pts
1100	8 pts
620	10 pts
850	4 pts
260	7 pts

double 170

halve 520

double 550

halve 1280

halve 540

double 670

halve 660

halve 1700

halve 1500

double 930

halve 820

double 240

double 480

double 310

double 830

double 720

halve 1840

halve 280

Teachers' note Encourage the children to recognise the links between doubling/halving a three-digit multiple of 10, for example 820, and doubling/halving a two-digit number, such as 82. The children should keep a record of their scores. They can use a calculator to check the answers. As an extension activity, ask them to investigate which spot answers do not appear on the tower.

**Developing Numeracy
Calculations Year 5
© A & C Black**

Cheque game

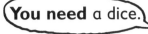

You need a dice.

- **This is a game for one player.**

☆ Cut out the cheques and spread them face down.

☆ Pick a cheque and roll a dice.

If the dice shows $\boxed{1}$, $\boxed{2}$ or $\boxed{3}$, **halve** the amount on the cheque.

If the dice shows $\boxed{4}$, $\boxed{5}$ or $\boxed{6}$, **double** the amount.

☆ Record the amount. After five turns find the total amount (your score).

☆ Repeat for the other five cheques. Which was your best score?

☆ Reshuffle the cheques and play again. Can you improve your score?

OHR Pay Winner four thousand, six hundred pounds	£4600 V. Rich	OHR Pay Winner three thousand, four hundred pounds	£3400 V. Rich
OHR Pay Winner one thousand, eight hundred pounds	£1800 V. Rich	OHR Pay Winner two thousand, four hundred pounds	£2400 V. Rich
OHR Pay Winner three thousand, six hundred pounds	£3600 V. Rich	OHR Pay Winner four thousand, eight hundred pounds	£4800 V. Rich
OHR Pay Winner six thousand pounds	£6000 V. Rich	OHR Pay Winner one thousand, two hundred pounds	£1200 V. Rich
OHR Pay Winner three thousand, two hundred pounds	£3200 V. Rich	OHR Pay Winner four thousand, four hundred pounds	£4400 V. Rich

Teachers' note Encourage the children to recognise the links between doubling/halving a multiple of 100, for example 4600, and doubling/halving a two-digit number, such as 46. Children can be asked to investigate what would be the maximum possible score in this activity, and the minimum. As a challenge, ask children to win £50 000 for charity and to record how many rounds they need to play.

Developing Numeracy Calculations Year 5 © A & C Black

Pocket pets

The toy shop stores pocket pets in boxes of 50 .

• Work out how many of each type of pet there are.

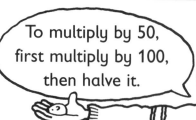

To multiply by 50, first multiply by 100, then halve it.

1.   34 boxes

Mice

34 x 50 = 1700

2.   46 boxes

Snakes

____ x ____ = ____

3.   82 boxes

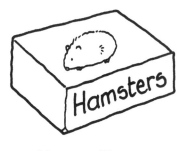

Hamsters

____ x ____ = ____

4.   65 boxes

Rabbits

____ x ____ = ____

5.   87 boxes

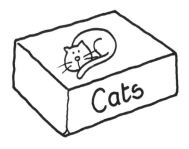

Cats

____ x ____ = ____

6.   19 boxes

Spiders

____ x ____ = ____

7.   51 boxes

Dogs

____ x ____ = ____

8.   35 boxes

Lizards

____ x ____ = ____

9.   27 boxes

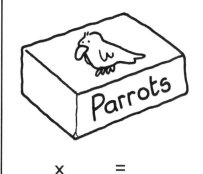

Parrots

____ x ____ = ____

Pocket pets sell for 50p   each.

• Find the value of the total number of:

mice £ _____   cats £ _____   dogs £ _____

Teachers' note Demonstrate to the children that the strategy of multiplying by 100 and then halving can be done the other way round (particularly on an even number), i.e. halve first, then multiply by 100.

**Developing Numeracy
Calculations Year 5**
© A & C Black

Stamp duty

• Complete the ☐x 8☐ table.

$1 \times 8 = \underline{8}$ $6 \times 8 = \underline{}$

$2 \times 8 = \underline{}$ $7 \times 8 = \underline{}$

$3 \times 8 = \underline{}$ $8 \times 8 = \underline{}$

$4 \times 8 = \underline{}$ $9 \times 8 = \underline{}$

$5 \times 8 = \underline{}$ $10 \times 8 = \underline{}$

• Use the answers in the table to help you find the cost of these stamps.

To work out 4 x 16, double the answer to 4 x 8.

1.
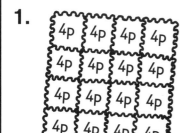

$4p \times 16 = \underline{64p}$

2.
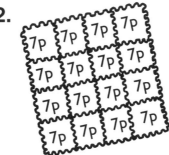

$7p \times 16 = \underline{}$

3.
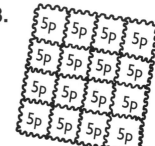

$5p \times 16 = \underline{}$

4.

$9p \times 16 = \underline{}$

5.

$6p \times 16 = \underline{}$

6.

$8p \times 16 = \underline{}$

• Write the cost of ☐32☐ of each stamp.

 6p

 9p

7p

$6p \times 32 = \underline{}$ $9p \times 32 = \underline{}$ $7p \times 32 = \underline{}$

Teachers' note The relationship between the multiples of numbers such as 4 and 2, 6 and 3, or 8 and 4 can be demonstrated on a multiplication square. Show that the rows of one multiple are double the numbers in the row of the other.

Developing Numeracy Calculations Year 5 © A & C Black

Keeping posted

- **Complete the table by doubling.**

Each letter needs a ☐ 23p ☐ stamp.

- **Find the cost of sending these piles of letters.**

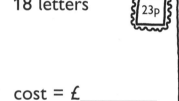

Show your workings.

Use the table to help you.

1 x 23 = __23__

2 x 23 = _____

4 x 23 = _____

8 x 23 = _____

16 x 23 = _____

1.

17 letters [23p]

$368 + 23 = 391$

cost = £__3.91__

2.

12 letters [23p]

cost = £_____

3.

24 letters [23p]

cost = £_____

4.

18 letters [23p]

cost = £_____

5.

14 letters [23p]

cost = £_____

6.

31 letters [23p]

cost = £_____

Now try this!

- **Complete the table by doubling.**

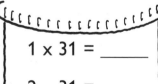

1 x 31 = _____

2 x 31 = _____

4 x 31 = _____

8 x 31 = _____

16 x 31 = _____

- **Use the table to solve these multiplications.**

17 x 31 = _____

20 x 31 = _____

9 x 31 = _____

13 x 31 = _____

Teachers' note Invite the children to explore how many different multiples of 23 they can find from the table at the top of the page.

**Developing Numeracy
Calculations Year 5
© A & C Black**

Multiplication crackers

• **Complete these multiplication tables.**

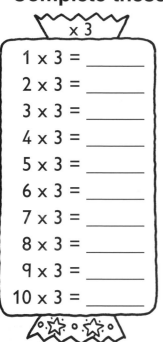

x 3

1 x 3 = _____
2 x 3 = _____
3 x 3 = _____
4 x 3 = _____
5 x 3 = _____
6 x 3 = _____
7 x 3 = _____
8 x 3 = _____
9 x 3 = _____
10 x 3 = _____

x 7

1 x 7 = _____
2 x 7 = _____
3 x 7 = _____
4 x 7 = _____
5 x 7 = _____
6 x 7 = _____
7 x 7 = _____
8 x 7 = _____
9 x 7 = _____
10 x 7 = _____

x 10

1 x 10 = _____
2 x 10 = _____
3 x 10 = _____
4 x 10 = _____
5 x 10 = _____
6 x 10 = _____
7 x 10 = _____
8 x 10 = _____
9 x 10 = _____
10 x 10 = _____

• **Use the tables above to complete these.**

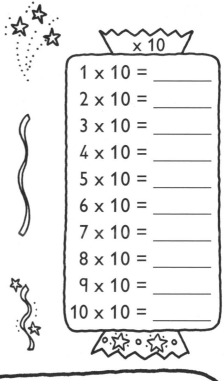

To find 7 x 13, add 7 x 3 = 21 and 7 x 10 = 70. So 7 x 13 = 91.

x 13

1 x 13 = _____
2 x 13 = _____
3 x 13 = _____
4 x 13 = _____
5 x 13 = _____
6 x 13 = _____
7 x 13 = _____
8 x 13 = _____
9 x 13 = _____
10 x 13 = _____

x 17

1 x 17 = _____
2 x 17 = _____
3 x 17 = _____
4 x 17 = _____
5 x 17 = _____
6 x 17 = _____
7 x 17 = _____
8 x 17 = _____
9 x 17 = _____
10 x 17 = _____

x 14

1 x 14 = _____
2 x 14 = _____
3 x 14 = _____
4 x 14 = _____
5 x 14 = _____
6 x 14 = _____
7 x 14 = _____
8 x 14 = _____
9 x 14 = _____
10 x 14 = _____

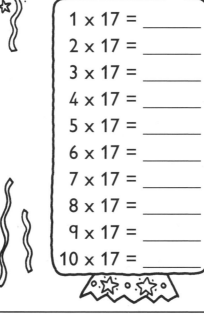

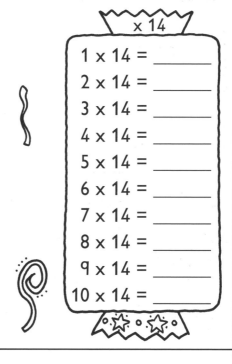

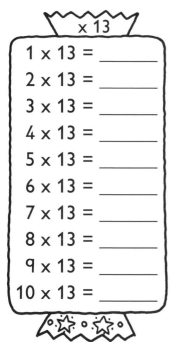

• **Use the tables above, and doubling, to complete these.**

16 x 17 = _____   14 x 13 = _____   18 x 14 = _____

12 x 14 = _____   16 x 13 = _____   18 x 17 = _____

Teachers' note This strategy can be demonstrated using known facts, for example, explain that 10 x 13 = 130 can be seen as the sum of 10 x 10 and 10 x 3. Children can develop this to confidently solve any multiplication problem, for example 23 x 37.

**Developing Numeracy
Calculations Year 5
© A & C Black**

Party bags

Sam buys $\boxed{21}$ of each gift for his party bags.

• **Find the total cost for each type of gift.**

Start by multiplying the cost by **20**.

1.

13 × 20 = __260__
13 × 21 = __273__
cost = £ __2.73__

$\boxed{13p}$

2.

stickers
17 × 20 = _____
17 × 21 = _____
cost = £ _____

$\boxed{17p}$

3.

I am
____ × ____ = ____
____ × ____ = ____
cost = £ _____

$\boxed{24p}$

4.
toffee
_____ = _____
_____ = _____
cost = £ _____

$\boxed{32p}$

• **Emma buys $\boxed{19}$ of each gift. Find the cost.**

5.
16 × 20 = __320__
16 × 19 = _____
cost = £ _____

$\boxed{16p}$

6.

_____ = ____
_____ = ____
cost = £ _____

$\boxed{35p}$

7.

chewies
_____ = ____
_____ = ____
cost = £ _____

$\boxed{28p}$

8.

_____ = ____
_____ = ____
cost = £ _____

$\boxed{23p}$

Now try this!

• **How much is a packet of crisps if $\boxed{21}$ packets cost $\boxed{£5.46}$ and $\boxed{19}$ packets cost $\boxed{£4.94}$?**

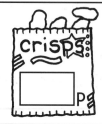
crisps

Teachers' note Before beginning the activity, remind the children of strategies for multiplying by 20, for example double first, then multiply by 10, or the reverse order. To prevent children from making mistakes when adjusting, ensure that they fully understand the process, for example, to work out 13 x 21 from 13 x 20, they need to add one more lot of 13.

**Developing Numeracy
Calculations Year 5
© A & C Black**

Mystery tour

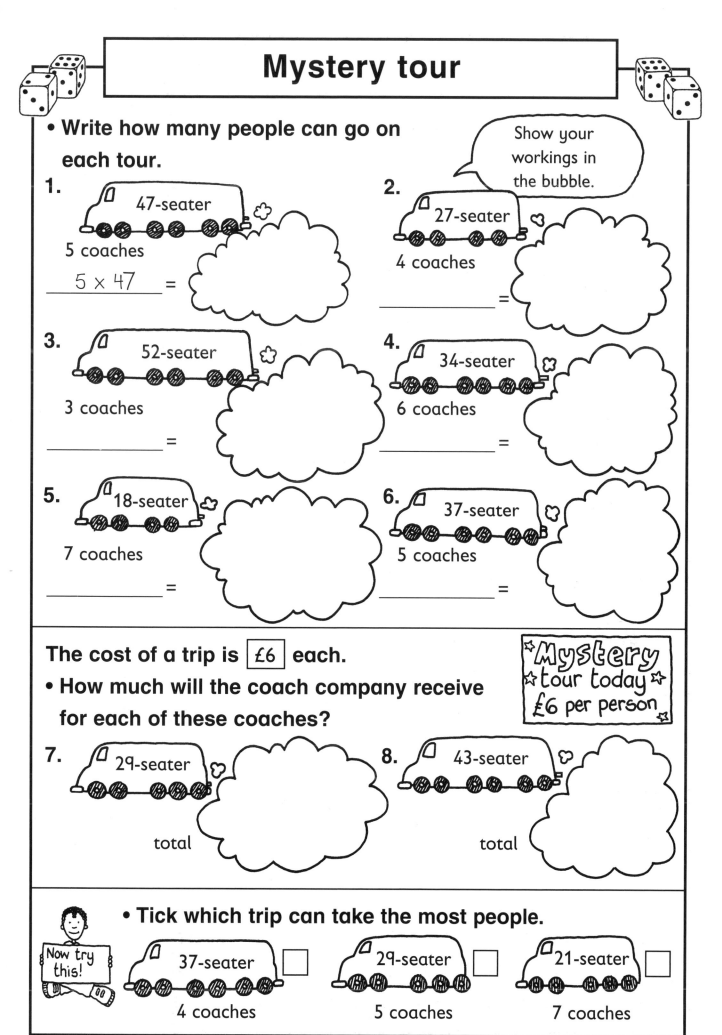

- **Write how many people can go on each tour.**

Show your workings in the bubble.

1. 47-seater
    5 coaches
    5 × 47 =

2. 27-seater
    4 coaches
    _____ =

3. 52-seater
    3 coaches
    _____ =

4. 34-seater
    6 coaches
    _____ =

5. 18-seater
    7 coaches
    _____ =

6. 37-seater
    5 coaches
    _____ =

The cost of a trip is ☐£6☐ each.

- **How much will the coach company receive for each of these coaches?**

Mystery tour today £6 per person

7. 29-seater
    total

8. 43-seater
    total

- **Tick which trip can take the most people.**

Now try this!

37-seater ☐
4 coaches

29-seater ☐
5 coaches

21-seater ☐
7 coaches

Teachers' note Stress the need to be secure in the quick recall of the multiplication facts up to 10 × 10 in order to calculate mentally: for example, to calculate 6 × 34 requires knowledge of 6 × 3 (leading to 6 × 30 = 180) plus 6 × 4. Similarly, to calculate 7 × 39 requires knowledge of 7 × 4 (leading to 7 × 40 = 280) minus 7 × 1.

**Developing Numeracy
Calculations Year 5
© A & C Black**

Magic multiplications

These six multiplications will help you
to answer all the other calculations.

$30 \times 15 = 450$ $16 \times 14 = 224$

$18 \times 12 = 216$ $23 \times 44 = 1012$

$48 \times 18 = 864$ $32 \times 16 = 512$

• **Complete the divisions.**

1. $224 \div 14 = $ ___16___   **2.** $864 \div 48 = $ _____

3. $1012 \div 44 = $ _____   **4.** $512 \div 16 = $ _____

5. $216 \div 12 = $ _____   **6.** $450 \div 15 = $ _____

• **Complete the calculations.**

7. $48 \times 180 = $ _____   **8.** $450 \div 150 = $ _____

9. $160 \times 14 = $ _____   **10.** $2160 \div 18 = $ _____

11. $230 \times 44 = $ _____   **12.** $5120 \div 16 = $ _____

13. $8640 \div 180 = $ _____   **14.** $2240 \div 140 = $ _____

• **Use the same six multiplications
to help you complete these.**

$224 \div 32 = $ _____ $16 \times 28 = $ _____

$864 \div 36 = $ _____ $512 \div 64 = $ _____

$18 \times 24 = $ _____ $44 \times 46 = $ _____

Use factors
to help you.
Example:
$\times 28$ is $\times 14$,
then $\times 2$.
$\div 32$ is $\div 16$,
then $\div 2$.

Teachers' note Encouraging children to read a division such as $224 \div 14$ as both '224 divided by 14' and 'How many 14s make 224?' will help to build security in relating multiplication and division facts.

**Developing Numeracy
Calculations Year 5**
© **A & C Black**

Flights

Here are some flight distances in miles.

Italy	France	Denmark	Portugal	Spain	Hungary	Germany	Belgium
900	300	400	800	700	600	500	200

These airlines make regular trips to the destinations.

• Write how many miles are covered.

30 trips to Denmark

$30 \times 400 =$

Airborn

70 trips to Belgium

50 trips to France

30 trips to Hungary

Top Cloud

50 trips to Germany

Go Away

40 trips to Denmark

---

cheap~air

60 trips to Spain

PLANE + simple

30 trips to Italy

PLANET AIR

80 trips to Portugal

• A plane has flown 42 000 miles . How many single trips can it have made to:

Spain?_____   France?_____   Belgium?_____   Hungary?_____

Now try this!

A plane has flown 24 000 miles . All its trips were the same distance. The distance was a multiple of 100 miles, and less than 1000 miles.

• Find all seven possible trips and distances.

Example: 240 trips of 100 miles

Teachers' note Help the children to recognise that 70 lots of 200 is the same as 7 lots of 2000. Alternatively, this can be worked out by saying, '10 lots of 200 is 2000, so 70 lots is 7 x 2000'. In the second part of the main activity, the children should count there and back as two separate trips.

Developing Numeracy
Calculations Year 5
© A & C Black

Power pack pets!

Each power pack has had its power [doubled].

• Write how many units of power each pack had [before] it was doubled.

1.
30

15

2. 60

3. 90

4.
140

5.
110

6.
80

7.
70

8. 220

9. 190

Here is the charger which doubles the power.

• Complete the tables.

[130] in

double

out [260]

In	130	250	285	170	265	240	135	215
Out	260							

In	325	450	415	375	465	380	470	435
Out								

Now try this!

• Write how many units of power these packs had [before] they were doubled.

190   330   550   690

Teachers' note Encourage the children to recognise that doubles of all multiples of 5 have a units digit of 0. One strategy for doubling a three-digit number, for example 265, is to partition it, double the parts, then combine. Another is to use known near doubles, for example double 250 = 500, and double 15 = 30, then combine.

**Developing Numeracy
Calculations Year 5
© A & C Black**

52

Battling robots

- **Play this game with a partner.**

☆ Cut out the robot cards and spread them face down.

☆ Let battle begin!

☆ Each player turns over a robot and says its **product**. The robot with the largest product wins the battle and the player keeps both robots. If the battle is a draw, each player keeps their own robot.

☆ The winner is the player who collects the most robots.

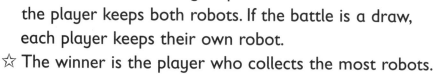

Check each other's answers.

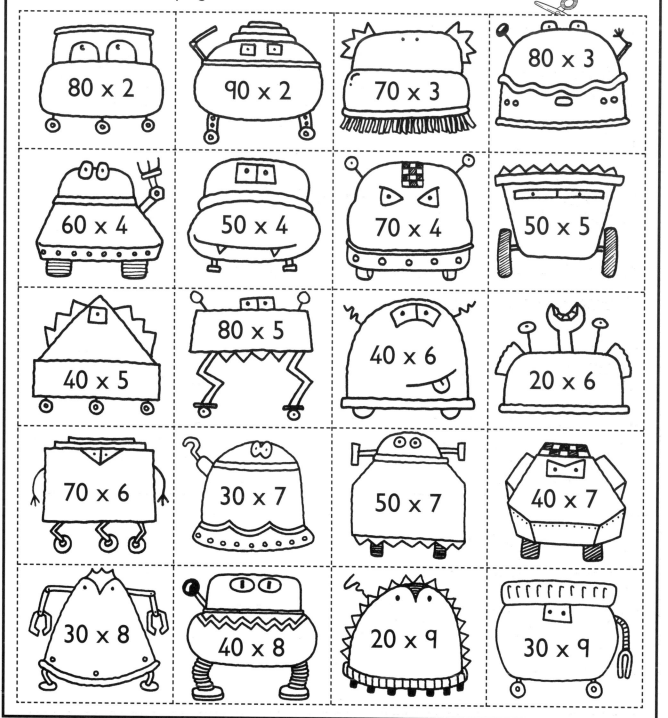

80 x 2 90 x 2 70 x 3 80 x 3

60 x 4 50 x 4 70 x 4 50 x 5

40 x 5 80 x 5 40 x 6 20 x 6

70 x 6 30 x 7 50 x 7 40 x 7

30 x 8 40 x 8 20 x 9 30 x 9

Teachers' note Encourage the children to recognise the links between multiplying a multiple of 10, for example 40 x 6, and multiplying single digits, such as 4 x 6. Quick mental calculation is dependent on quick recall of the multiplication facts up to 10 x 10. As a variation of the game, children could work through the questions individually against the clock and then check their answers with a calculator.

**Developing Numeracy
Calculations Year 5**
© A & C Black

Dice challenge

- **Roll a dice. Choose any multiplication and write the dice number as the tens digit. Then write the answer.**

Challenge: When you choose where to write the digit, try to make an answer **between 100 and 200**. Do this for as many as you can out of 10.

You need a dice.

4 | 4 x 3 = __132__

7 x 2 = _____

3 x 4 = _____

4 x 3 = _____

2 x 6 = _____

5 x 4 = _____

4 x 5 = _____

3 x 7 = _____

6 x 2 = _____

score _____ 1 0

3 x 5 = _____

Now try this!

- **Write a tens digit in each calculation to make an answer** | between 50 and 100 | **. Write the answers.**

1. ☐ 4 x 3 = ____   **2.** ☐ 4 x 4 = ____   **3.** ☐ 5 x 5 = ____

4. ☐ 2 x 6 = ____   **5.** ☐ 7 x 2 = ____   **6.** ☐ 3 x 7 = ____

Teachers' note The children could investigate which dice numbers will fit into each multiplication in order to arrive at a product between 100 and 200.

Developing Numeracy Calculations Year 5 © A & C Black

54

Grid multiplying

- Use the grids to help you complete the multiplications.
- Make an estimate first.

1.   432 x 6

	400	30	2		estimate
6	2400	180	12	= 2592	2400

2.   183 x 4

estimate

= _____

3.   251 x 3

estimate

= _____

4.   357 x 5

estimate

= _____

5.   624 x 4

estimate

= _____

6.   258 x 6

estimate

= _____

7.   462 x 5

estimate

= _____

8.   138 x 7

estimate

= _____

Now try this!

- Now calculate the difference between your estimate and the answer.

1. _____   2. _____

3. _____   4. _____

5. _____   6. _____

7. _____   8. _____

Teachers' note Remind the children how to round a three-digit number to the nearest hundred so that they can use this to estimate the products, for example 183 x 4 is approximately 200 x 4 = 800. A more sophisticated method is to recognise that the answer will be approximately 80 less than this, i.e. 720.

**Developing Numeracy
Calculations Year 5
© A & C Black**

More grid multiplying

- **Use the grids to help you complete the multiplications.**
- **Make an estimate first.**

1.   43 × 27

	40	3
20	800	60
7	280	21

estimate
1200

```
  860
+ 301
------
 1161
```

2.   29 × 32

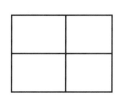

estimate

+ ....

3.   54 × 26

estimate

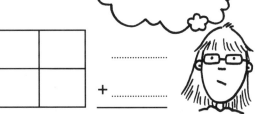

+ ....

4.   73 × 19

estimate

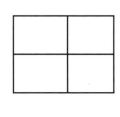

+ ....

5.   46 × 44

estimate

+ ....

6.   32 × 24

estimate

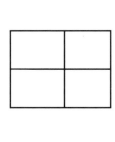
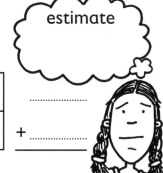

+ ....

Now try this!

- **Which multiplications are shown by these grids?**

_____ x _____

200	30
100	15

_____ x _____

600	80
90	12

Teachers' note In order to make estimates, the children can round each two-digit number to the nearest 10, then multiply these together. For children who struggle with the extension activity, suggest that they look at the smallest number first, for example 15, and try out factors of that number. As a further extension, they could work out grids for a partner to find the multiplications.

**Developing Numeracy
Calculations Year 5
© A & C Black**

- **Mark these pieces of homework.**
  ✓ or ✗
- **Ring any errors.**

Name: **Narinder Kaur**

3 4 6	2 5 8
x 9	x 7
3 1 1 4	1 8 0 6
4 5	4 5

7 3 2	1 9 6
x 4	x 6
2 7 2 8	1 1 7 6
1	5 3

5 4 4	4 7 1
x 3	x 5
1 6 2 2	2 3 5 5
1 1	3

mark / 6

Name: **Declan O'Hara**

1 7 4	3 1 7
x 6	x 5
1 0 4 4	1 5 8 5
4 2	3

2 8 3	4 4 3
x 4	x 5
1 1 3 2	2 2 2 5
3 1	2 2

5 4 2	6 4 7
x 6	x 3
3 2 5 2	1 9 5 1
2 1	1 2

mark / 6

- **Complete these multiplications.**
- **Ask a partner to check for any errors.**

2 6 8	3 2 5	4 4 6
x 6	x 7	x 5
_____	_____	_____

Teachers' note In order to find the mistakes, the children need to work through each calculation themselves. Some may benefit from writing out the calculations on a separate piece of paper, making a new row for each part of the multiplication, then adding these parts together.

**Developing Numeracy
Calculations Year 5
© A & C Black**

Decimal multiplication

nate for each multiplication.

	4·8 x 3	3·6 x 4	5·9 x 5	1·8 x 8	2·3 x 7	3·3 x 5
	15					
Answer	14·4					

- **Complete each multiplication below.**
- **Write the answers in the grid above.**

1.

$$4·8 \times 3$$

| 12·0 | 4·0 x 3 |
| 2·4 | 0·8 x 3 |

14·4

2.

$$3·6 \times 4$$

| | 3·0 x 4 |
| | 0·6 x 4 |

3.

$$5·9 \times 5$$

| | 5·0 x 5 |
| | 0·9 x 5 |

4.

$$1·8 \times 8$$

.... x 8

.... x 8

5.

$$2·3 \times 7$$

.... x ....

.... x ....

6.

$$3·3 \times 5$$

.... x ....

.... x ....

- **For which multiplication was your estimate the closest?** _____

Now try this!

- **Shuffle number cards** 1 **to** 9. ▢.▢ x ▢
- **Deal three cards.**
- **Write the numbers in the boxes. Complete the multiplication.**

.... x ....

.... x ....

_____

_____

Teachers' note Explain to the children how to make estimates, for example for 2·3 x 7, they should round the decimal number to the nearest whole number, which gives approximately 2 x 7 = 14 (but the product will be a little more than 14 because 2·3 is a little more than 2). Provide number cards for the extension (see page 61). The children can repeat this several times, recording on a separate sheet.

**Developing Numeracy
Calculations Year 5
© A & C Black**

Addressing division

• **Complete these divisions. Estimate first.**

1. $115 \div 5$

estimate **20**

$5\overline{)115}$

$-100 \quad 20 \times 5$

15

$-15 \quad 3 \times 5$

0

answer **23**

2. $144 \div 6$

estimate

$6\overline{)144}$

$-\underline{} \quad 20 \times 6$

$-\underline{} \quad 4 \times 6$

answer ....

3. $126 \div 7$

estimate

$7\overline{)126}$

$-\underline{} \quad \text{......} \times 7$

$-\underline{} \quad \text{......} \times 7$

answer ....

4. $204 \div 6$

estimate

$6\overline{)204}$

$-\underline{} \quad \text{......} \times \text{.....}$

$-\underline{} \quad \text{......} \times \text{.....}$

answer ....

5. $144 \div 4$

estimate

$4\overline{)144}$

$-\underline{} \quad \text{......} \times \text{.....}$

$-\underline{} \quad \text{......} \times \text{.....}$

answer ....

6. $368 \div 8$

estimate

$8\overline{)368}$

$-\underline{} \quad \text{......} \times \text{.....}$

$-\underline{} \quad \text{......} \times \text{.....}$

answer ....

• **Complete these divisions. Each has a** ⟨remainder⟩.

7. $178 \div 5$

estimate

$\overline{)}$

$-\underline{} \quad \text{......} \times \text{.....}$

$-\underline{} \quad \text{......} \times \text{.....}$

answer .... r ....

8. $239 \div 6$

estimate

$\overline{)}$

$-\underline{} \quad \text{......} \times \text{.....}$

$-\underline{} \quad \text{......} \times \text{.....}$

answer .... r ....

9. $193 \div 4$

estimate

$\overline{)}$

$-\underline{} \quad \text{......} \times \text{.....}$

$-\underline{} \quad \text{......} \times \text{.....}$

answer .... r ....

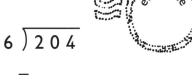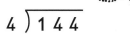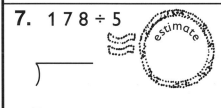

Teachers' note Explain this method to the children: for example, when dividing by 6, the first stage is to subtract as many tens of 6 as possible and the next stage is to subtract as many units of 6 as possible. To make an estimate of 144 ÷ 6, the children should search for a number near to 144 which is divisible by 6, such as 120 (20 x 6).

**Developing Numeracy
Calculations Year 5
© A & C Black**

Odd-Bod and Even-Steven

• **Play this game with a partner.**

O stands for **odd**.

E stands for **even**.

☆ Decide who is going to be 'odd' and who will be 'even'.
☆ Cut out the cards and spread them face down.
☆ Take turns to reveal a card. If it is yours (for example, if you are 'odd' and the answer is odd), keep the card. If not, give it to your partner.
☆ Check each other's answers.
☆ The winner is the first to collect eight cards.

307 + 199 + 535	185 + 454 + 313	493 + 352 + 176
517 + 193 + 205	29 + 77 + 45 + 61	28 + 56 + 70 + 93
45 + 49 + 51 + 52	39 + 38 + 26 + 24	35 + 41 + 28 + 32
269 – 175	438 – 215	O + O + E
O + O + O	E – E	O – O
O + E + E	O + E + E + E	O + O + E + E

Teachers' note Follow up the activity by inviting the children to find out how many of the cards have an odd answer and how many an even answer. Ask them whether there is any advantage in being 'odd' or 'even'. Some children may need to test the general cases, for example O + O + O, by trying out specific examples.

**Developing Numeracy
Calculations Year 5
© A & C Black**

Number cards

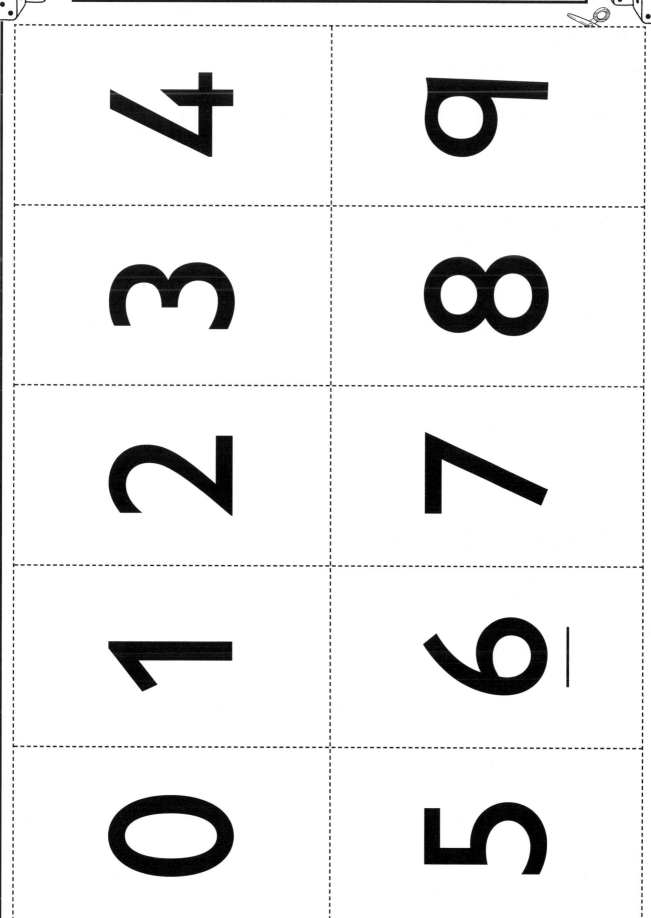

4   9

3   8

2   7

1   6

0   5

Teachers' note These number cards can be copied onto card and used with the extension activity on page 58.

Developing Numeracy
Calculations Year 5
© A & C Black

p 6
cake 45p, sandwich 21p, apple 82p,
choc bar 69p, chips 76p, burger 14p,
bun 54p, yoghurt 57p, juice 36p

Coins used for change	Cost of item
50p 10p 2p	38p
50p 5p	45p
20p 5p 10p 1p	64p

Coins used for change	Cost of item
20p 10p 5p	65p
20p 10p 10p 1p	59p
10p 2p 1p	87p

Now try this!
48 and 52　　36 and 64　　42 and 58

p 7
1. 800 ml　　**2.** 300 ml　　**3.** 350 ml
4. 850 ml　　**5.** 150 ml　　**6.** 650 ml
7. 450 ml　　**8.** 200 ml
9. 550 ml　　**10.** 350 ml
11. 450 ml　　**12.** 450 ml

Now try this!
225 ml

p 9
1. 219　　2. 314　　3. 226
4. 4013　　5. 4016　　6. 4028

Now try this!
129　　335　　527　　6538

p 11
1. 3·1 kg　　**2.** 5·3 kg　　**3.** 11·5 kg
4. 7·4 kg　　**5.** 13·8 kg　　**6.** 11·2 kg
7. 9·2 kg　　**8.** 15·4 kg　　**9.** 19·1 kg

Now try this!
4·1 kg and 4·2 kg　　2·8 kg and 3·0 kg　　6·1 kg and 6·4 kg

p 12
1. £418　　**2.** £235　　**3.** £499
4. £429　　**5.** £482　　**6.** £622
7. £422　　**8.** £339
9. £213　　**10.** £413

Now try this!
TV £213　　　　recorder £71

p 13
1. 243 + 138 = 381
2. 362 + 246 = 608 **or** 138 + 246 = 384
3. 214 + 148 = 362
4. 246 + 362 = 608
5. 381 − 243 = 138
6. 381 − 138 = 243 **or** 384 − 138 = 246
7. 362 − 214 = 148
8. 608 − 246 = 362
9. 381 − 138 = 243
10. 384 − 138 = 246 **or** 384 − 246 = 138
11. 362 − 214 = 148 **or** 362 − 148 = 214
12. 608 − 362 = 246 **or** 384 − 138 = 246

Now try this!
Possibilities include:
213 + 345 = 558　　558 − 345 = 213　　558 − 213 = 345
213 + 96 = 309　　309 − 96 = 213　　309 − 213 = 96
345 + 213 = 558　　96 + 213 = 309

p 14
blue　　4 + 2 + 7 + 9 = 22
green　6 + 5 + 9 + 9 + 3 = 32
grey　　6 + 5 + 9 + 7 = 27
yellow 7 + 9 + 2 + 2 + 7 + 11 = 38
black　4 + 2 + 9 + 8 + 4 = 27

red　　5 + 9 + 4 = 18
pink　　5 + 8 + 3 + 4 = 20
orange 7 + 5 + 9 + 3 + 6 + 9 = 39
white 11 + 5 + 8 + 6 + 9 = 39
purple　5 + 7 + 5 + 5 + 2 + 9 = 33

cone　　8 + 7 + 3 + 9 = 27
cube　　8 + 7 + 4 + 9 = 28
square 7 + 3 + 7 + 9 + 5 + 9 = 40

p 15
Solutions include:

1.
40	60
70	

2.
	20
70	70

3.
90	30
20	

4.
60	90
	50

5.
90	
90	20

6.
80	70
40	

7.
70	50
	60

8.
	40
40	30

Now try this!

80	70
40	90

20	50
70	80

p 16
1. 74　　**2.** 75　　**3.** 77
4. 77　　**5.** 74　　**6.** 89
7. 80　　**8.** 110　　**9.** 100

p 17
1. 3 × 15 = 45　　　　**2.** 3 × 32 = 96
3. 3 × 20 = 60　　　　**4.** 3 × 50 = 150
5. 4 × 30 = 120　　　**6.** 4 × 50 = 200
7. 5 × 10 = 50　　　　**8.** 5 × 40 = 200
9. 12　　　　　　　　　**10.** 47
11. 24　　　　　　　　**12.** 30
13. 40, 40 **or** 39, 41 **or** 38, 42　　**14.** 30, 34

p 18
710　　610　　920
410　　610　　720
190　　330　　170

Now try this!
350 adults　280 children　£3150

p 19

300	200	400	**900**
100	500	600	**1200**
800	700	900	**2400**
1200	**1400**	**1900**	

400	700	600	400	**2100**
500	300	500	100	**1400**
700	400	200	600	**1900**
300	200	500	300	**1300**
1900	**1600**	**1800**	**1400**	

900	700	300	1900
200	100	600	900
500	**800**	400	1700
1600	**1600**	**1300**	

100	**800**	200	**1100**
300	500	400	**1200**
400	300	**200**	**900**
800	1600	800	

Now try this!

800	100	**600**
300	**500**	**700**
400	**900**	200

p 21
1. 595　　**2.** 894　　**3.** 395
4. 588　　**5.** 595
6. 677　　**7.** 496
8. 312　　**9.** 335　　**10.** 137

Now try this!
home　　away
390　　　370

home　　away
475　　　455

p 22

1. 734 + 66 = 800 **2.** 463 + 37 = 500 **3.** 275 + 25 = 300
4. 583 + 17 = 600 **5.** 369 + 31 = 400 **6.** 838 + 62 = 900
7. 753 **8.** 332 **9.** 427

Now try this!
scores:
Khalid 648   Jill 583   Lee 721
differences:
73   65   138

p 24

1. £22 **2.** £103
3. £37 **4.** £113 **5.** £112
6. £6897 **7.** £3896 **8.** £5895

Now try this!
£3960   £5940   £891

p 25

1. 8·3 cm **2.** 4·1 cm **3.** 5·3 cm
4. 9·3 cm **5.** 9·4 cm **6.** 6·3 cm
7. 3·7 cm **8.** 5·7 cm **9.** 5·6 cm
10. 3·6 cm **11.** 4·7 cm **12.** 3·6 cm

p 26

1. 7197 **2.** 5295 **3.** 8024 **4.** 6961 **5.** 8252

Now try this!
15 903

p 28

1.
$$4325 + 2164 = 6489$$
2.
$$3752 + 4465 = 8217$$
3.
$$4862 + 3715 = 8577$$

4.
$$2938 + 4271 = 7209$$
5.
$$2663 + 3518 = 6181$$
6.
$$4792 + 1936 = 6728$$

7.
$$5843 + 2169 = 8012$$
8.
$$4385 + 4673 = 9058$$
9.
$$2594 + 1389 = 3983$$

p 30

1. 458 **2.** 259
3. 254 **4.** 545
5. 485 **6.** 158

Now try this!
545 − 158 = 387

p 31

1.
543 − 189 = 354
= 500 + 40 + 3
100 + 80 + 9
= 500 + 30 + 13
100 + 80 + 9
= 400 + 130 + 13
100 + 80 + 9
300 + 50 + 4

2.
632 − 275 = 357
= 600 + 30 + 2
200 + 70 + 5
= 600 + 20 + 12
200 + 70 + 5
= 500 + 120 + 12
200 + 70 + 5
300 + 50 + 7

3.
944 − 377 = 567
= 900 + 40 + 4
300 + 70 + 7
= 900 + 30 + 14
300 + 70 + 7
= 800 + 130 + 14
300 + 70 + 7
500 + 60 + 7

4.
855 − 386 = 469
= 800 + 50 + 5
300 + 80 + 6
= 800 + 40 + 15
300 + 80 + 6
= 700 + 140 + 15
300 + 80 + 6
400 + 60 + 9

5.
672 − 158 = 514
= 600 + 70 + 2
100 + 50 + 8
= 600 + 60 + 12
100 + 50 + 8
500 + 10 + 4

6.
513 − 279 = 234
= 500 + 10 + 3
200 + 70 + 9
= 500 + 0 + 13
200 + 70 + 9
= 400 + 100 + 13
200 + 70 + 9
200 + 30 + 4

p 32

The following subtractions are incorrect:

1.
$$6\overset{7}{\cancel{8}}\overset{1}{1} - 135 = \boxed{4}46$$
5.
$$\overset{8}{\cancel{9}}1\overset{1}{3} - 482 = 4\boxed{2}1$$
7.
$$\boxed{5}4\overset{1}{1} - 129 = 432$$
9.
$$\boxed{4}\overset{4}{\cancel{5}}\overset{1}{2} - 166 = 386$$
11.
$$\overset{3}{\cancel{4}}\overset{1}{3}\overset{2}{\cancel{3}}2 - 286 = 1\boxed{3}6$$

Now try this!
A: 321 **B:** 287
B is closer to 300.

p 33

S 12·9 **H** 27·6
E 33·8 **R** 34·8
E 54·5 **P** 16·4
The shape name is **SPHERE**.

Now try this!
54·5 − 27·6 = 26·9   33·8 − 12·9 = 20·9   34·8 − 16·4 = 18·4

p 34

1. (3 + 5) × 2 = 16 **2.** (5 × 6) + 2 = 32
3. (5 + 6) × 3 = 33 **4.** (3 × 5) − 2 = 13 **or** (6 × 3) − 5 = 13
5. 6 + (2 × 3) = 12 **6.** 5 + (6 × 3) = 23
7. (2 × 3) + (5 × 6) = 36 **8.** (5 + 2) × 6 = 42
9. (3 × 5) − 6 = 9
  or (6 × 2) − 3 = 9 **10.** (5 + 2 + 3) × 6 = 60

p 35

1. 46 ÷ 5 = $9\frac{1}{5}$ **2.** 35 ÷ 6 = $5\frac{5}{6}$ **3.** 28 ÷ 3 = $9\frac{1}{3}$
4. 24 ÷ 7 = $3\frac{3}{7}$ **5.** 43 ÷ 8 = $5\frac{3}{8}$ **6.** 29 ÷ 4 = $7\frac{1}{4}$
7. 23 **8.** 37 **9.** 15
10. 25 **11.** 13 **12.** 35

p 38

1.

2.

p 39

1. 25 m² **2.** 4 m² **3.** 49 m²
4. 9 m² **5.** 100 m² **6.** 64 m²
7. 16 m² **8.** 36 m² **9.** 81 m²

Now try this!
1. 51 **2.** 75 **3.** 64
4. 19 **5.** 36 **6.** 84

p 41

Board 1	Board 2	Board 3
103	183	59
109	151	168
203	81	127

Now try this!

Board 1		Board 2		Board 3	
65	130	73	146	82	164
83	166	54	108	61	122
56	112	63	126	75	150
71	142	81	162	57	114

Highest score possible with 3 darts:
Board 1 498   Board 2 486   Board 3 492

p 44

1. 34 × 50 = 1700 **2.** 46 × 50 = 2300 **3.** 82 × 50 = 4100
4. 65 × 50 = 3250 **5.** 87 × 50 = 4350 **6.** 19 × 50 = 950
7. 51 × 50 = 2550 **8.** 35 × 50 = 1750 **9.** 27 × 50 = 1350

Now try this!
mice £850   cats £2175   dogs £1275

p 45
1. 64p
2. 112p or £1.12
3. 80p
4. 144p or £1.44
5. 96p
6. 128p or £1.28

Now try this!
192p or £1.92   288p or £2.88   224p or £2.24

p 46
1. 368 + 23 = 391, cost = £3.91
2. 184 + 92 = 276, cost = £2.76
3. 368 + 184 = 552, cost = £5.52
4. 368 + 46 = 414, cost = £4.14
5. 184 + 92 + 46 = 322 **or** 368 − 46 = 322, cost = £3.22
6. 368 + 184 + 92 + 46 + 23 = 713 **or** 368 + 368 − 23 = 713, cost = £7.13

Now try this!
17 × 31 = 496 + 31 = 527
20 × 31 = 496 + 124 = 620
9 × 31 = 248 + 31 = 279
13 × 31 = 248 + 124 + 31 = 403

p 47
x13	x17	x14
13	17	14
26	34	28
39	51	42
52	68	56
65	85	70
78	102	84
91	119	98
104	136	112
117	153	126
130	170	140

Now try this!
16 × 17 = 272   14 × 13 = 182   18 × 14 = 252
12 × 14 = 168   16 × 13 = 208   18 × 17 = 306

p 48
1. 13 × 20 = 260, 13 × 21 = 273, cost = £2.73
2. 17 × 20 = 340, 17 × 21 = 357, cost = £3.57
3. 24 × 20 = 480, 24 × 21 = 504, cost = £5.04
4. 32 × 20 = 640, 32 × 21 = 672, cost = £6.72
5. 16 × 20 = 320, 16 × 19 = 304, cost = £3.04
6. 35 × 20 = 700, 35 × 19 = 665, cost = £6.65
7. 28 × 20 = 560, 28 × 19 = 532, cost = £5.32
8. 23 × 20 = 460, 23 × 19 = 437, cost = £4.37

Now try this!
26p

p 49
1. 235
2. 108
3. 156
4. 204
5. 126
6. 185
7. £174
8. £258

Now try this!
37 × 4 = 148   29 × 5 = 145   21 × 7 = 147
The 37-seater coaches will take the most people.

p 50
1. 16
2. 18
3. 23
4. 32
5. 18
6. 30
7. 8640
8. 3
9. 2240
10. 120
11. 10120
12. 320
13. 48
14. 16

Now try this!
224 ÷ 32 = 7   16 × 28 = 448
864 ÷ 36 = 24   512 ÷ 64 = 8
18 × 24 = 432   44 × 46 = 2024

p 51
12000	14000	15000
18000	25000	16000
42000	27000	64000

60   140   210   70

Now try this!
240 × 100   120 × 200   80 × 300   60 × 400   48 × 500
40 × 600   30 × 800

p 52
1. 15
2. 30
3. 45
4. 70
5. 55
6. 40
7. 35
8. 110
9. 95

In	130	250	285	170	265	240	135	215
Out	260	500	570	340	530	480	270	430

In	325	450	415	375	465	380	470	435
Out	650	900	830	750	930	760	940	870

Now try this!
95   165   275   345

p 54
Now try this!
1. 24 × 3 = 72   2. 14 × 4 = 56 **or** 24 × 4 = 96   3. 15 × 5 = 75
4. 12 × 6 = 72
5. 27 × 2 = 54 **or** 37 × 2 = 74 **or** 47 × 2 = 94
6. 13 × 7 = 91

p 55
1. 2592
2. 732
3. 753
4. 1785
5. 2496
6. 1548
7. 2310
8. 966

p 56
1. 1161
2. 928
3. 1404
4. 1387
5. 2024
6. 768

Now try this!
23 × 15   34 × 23

p 57
The following multiplications are incorrect:

```
              7 3 2              5 4 4
          ×       4          ×       3
Narinder  ───────────        ───────────      4/6
          2 ⑦ 2 8            1 6 ② 2
              1                  1 1
```

```
              4 4 3              6 4 7
          ×       5          ×       3
Declan    ───────────        ───────────      4/6
          2 2 ② 5            1 9 ⑤ 1
              2 ②                1 2
```

Now try this!
```
   268          325          446
 ×   6        ×   7        ×   5
 ──────       ──────       ──────
  1608         2275         2230
   4 4          1 3          2 3
```

p 58
1. 14·4
2. 14·4
3. 29·5
4. 14·4
5. 16·1
6. 16·5

p 59
1. 23
2. 24
3. 18
4. 34
5. 36
6. 46
7. 35 r3
8. 39 r5
9. 48 r1